**FRIENDS OF ACPL**

Y0-DEW-479

### Date Due

| JAN 13 1955 | Alvite Twp. |
| | Borden |
| NOV 10 1955 | |
| MAY 3 1957 | |
| 3-20 | |
| | |
| | |
| | C. R |
| C. R | |

LET'S-READ-TOGETHER POEMS

# *Let's-Read-Together*

# POEMS

*An Anthology of Verse for Choral Reading*

*in*

*Kindergarten and Primary Grades*

SELECTED AND TESTED BY

HELEN A. BROWN
Washington Irving Elementary School
Syracuse, New York

and

HARRY J. HELTMAN
Director, School of Speech and Dramatic Art and Speech Clinic
Syracuse University

ROW, PETERSON AND COMPANY

Evanston, Illinois            White Plains, New York

*Copyright, 1949*
*Row, Peterson and Company*
3505

PRINTED IN THE UNITED STATES OF AMERICA

## CONTENTS

| | Page |
|---|---|
| Something About This Book | 1 |
| A Word About Choral Reading | 2 |
| Procedures | 3 |

### NURSERY RHYMES

| | |
|---|---|
| Baa, Baa, Black Sheep | 17 |
| Hickory Dickory Dock | 17 |
| A Farmer Went Riding | 17 |
| Goosie Gander | 18 |
| Hey Diddle Diddle | 19 |
| Humpty Dumpty | 19 |
| I Had a Little Pony | 19 |
| Jack and Jill | 20 |
| One, Two, Buckle My Shoe | 20 |
| Little Bo-Peep | 21 |
| Little Boy Blue | 21 |
| Little Jack Horner | 22 |
| Little Miss Muffet | 22 |
| Mistress Mary | 23 |
| Lucy Locket | 23 |
| Tom, Tom, the Piper's Son | 23 |
| Ride-a-Cock Horse | 24 |
| Mary Had a Little Lamb | 24 |
| Mix a Pancake | 25 |
| Ding Dong Bell | 25 |
| Old King Cole | 26 |

v

|  | Page |
|---|---|
| Sing a Song of Sixpence | 27 |
| Some Little Mice | 27 |
| Pease Porridge Hot | 28 |
| There Was a Crooked Man | 28 |
| When I Was a Little Boy | 29 |
| Pat-a-Cake | 30 |

## CHILDHOOD MYSTERY AND EXPERIENCE

| | |
|---|---|
| The Cupboard, *Walter de la Mare* | 32 |
| Bridges, *Rhoda W. Bacmeister* | 33 |
| About Buttons, *Dorothy Aldis* | 33 |
| Echo, *Author Unknown* | 34 |
| Everybody Says, *Dorothy Aldis* | 35 |
| Galoshes, *Rhoda W. Bacmeister* | 35 |
| Growing Up, *Author Unknown* | 36 |
| Hiding, *Dorothy Aldis* | 36 |
| Merry-Go-Round, *Dorothy W. Baruch* | 38 |
| Icy, *Rhoda W. Bacmeister* | 39 |
| Lullaby, *Sarah Jane S. Harrington* | 39 |
| Five Years Old, *Marie Louise Allen* | 40 |
| Milking Time, *Elizabeth Madox Roberts* | 41 |
| Mud, *Polly Chase Boyden* | 42 |
| My Funny Umbrella, *Alice Wilkins* | 42 |
| My Shadow, *Robert Louis Stevenson* | 43 |
| My Zipper Suit, *Marie Louise Allen* | 44 |
| My Kite, *Barbara and Beatrice Brown* | 44 |
| Naughty Soap Song, *Dorothy Aldis* | 45 |
| New Shoes, *Alice Wilkins* | 45 |
| The Park, *James S. Tippett* | 46 |

|   |   | Page |
|---|---|---|
| Sprinkling, *Dorothy Mason Pierce* | . . . . . | 46 |
| Hair Ribbons, *Author Unknown* | . . . . . | 47 |
| Boots, Boots, Boots, *Leroy F. Jackson* | . . . | 47 |
| Troubles, *Dorothy Aldis* | . . . . . . | 48 |
| Rocking Horse, *H. N. Bialik* | . . . . . | 48 |
| A Pop Corn Song, *Nancy Byrd Turner* | . . . . | 49 |
| See-Saw, *H. N. Bialik* | . . . . . . . | 50 |
| Seesaw, *Evelyn Beyer* | . . . . . . . | 51 |
| The Secret, *Author Unknown* | . . . . . | 51 |
| "Sh," *James S. Tippett* | . . . . . . . | 52 |
| Skyscrapers, *Rachel Field* | . . . . . . | 53 |
| Smells (Junior), *Christopher Morley* | . . . . | 54 |
| Soap Bubbles, *Author Unknown* | . . . . . | 54 |
| Sneezing, *Marie Louise Allen* | . . . . . | 55 |
| Spinning Top, *Frank Dempster Sherman* | . . . | 55 |
| Hippity Hop to Bed, *Leroy F. Jackson* | . . . . | 56 |
| Whistle, *Author Unknown* | . . . . . . | 56 |
| The Little Dreamer, *Old Rhyme* | . . . . . | 57 |
| Who's In, *Elizabeth Fleming* | . . . . . | 57 |

## LIVING THINGS

| Bird's Nest, *H. N. Bialik* | . . . . . . | 61 |
|---|---|---|
| The Chickens, *Anonymous* | . . . . . . | 61 |
| Crickets, *Helen Wing* | . . . . . . . | 62 |
| Tracks, *John Farrar* | . . . . . . . | 63 |
| Little Bug, *Rhoda W. Bacmeister* | . . . . . | 63 |
| The Duck, *Edith King* | . . . . . . . | 64 |
| Familiar Friends, *James S. Tippett* | . . . . | 65 |
| Fireflies, *Grace Wilson Coplen* | . . . . . | 66 |

|  | Page |
|---|---|
| THE GOLDFISH, *Dorothy Aldis* | 66 |
| GOOD MORNING, *Muriel Sipe* | 67 |
| I LOVE LITTLE PUSSY, *Jane Taylor* | 68 |
| THE HOUSE CAT, *Annette Wynne* | 69 |
| MRS. PECK-PIGEON, *Eleanor Farjeon* | 69 |
| KITTEN'S NIGHT THOUGHTS, *Oliver Herford* | 70 |
| THE KITTY, *Elizabeth Prentiss* | 71 |
| MICE, *Rose Fyleman* | 72 |
| MARY MIDDLING, *Rose Fyleman* | 73 |
| MOUSE, *Hilda Conkling* | 73 |
| THE MILKMAN'S HORSE, *Author Unknown* | 74 |
| MORAL SONG, *John Farrar* | 74 |
| MY DOG, *Marchette Gaylord Chute* | 75 |
| ONCE I SAW A LITTLE BIRD, *Author Unknown* | 76 |
| THE NAUGHTY LITTLE ROBIN, *Phoebe Cary* | 77 |
| THE PIGEONS, *Maud Burnham* | 78 |
| THE NEW BABY CALF, *Edith H. Newlin* | 78 |
| THE RABBIT, *Edith King* | 80 |
| ROBIN, *Tom Robinson* | 81 |
| PRECOCIOUS PIGGY, *Thomas Hood* | 82 |
| THE QUARRELSOME KITTENS, *Anonymous* | 84 |
| THE SWALLOW, *Christina Rossetti* | 85 |
| THE SQUIRREL, *Author Unknown* | 85 |
| THE ROBIN, *Laurence Alma-Tadema* | 86 |
| RABBITS, *Dorothy Baruch* | 87 |
| THE LITTLE TURTLE, *Vachel Lindsay* | 88 |
| WILD BEASTS, *Evaleen Stein* | 88 |
| TIME TO RISE, *R. L. Stevenson* | 89 |
| WHAT DOES LITTLE BIRDIE SAY?, *Alfred Tennyson* | 89 |

|  | Page |
|---|---|
| THREE LITTLE KITTENS, *Eliza Lee Follen* | 90 |
| THE WOODPECKER, *Elizabeth Madox Roberts* | 91 |

## NATURE AND SEASONS

|  |  |
|---|---|
| COVER, *Frances M. Frost* | 95 |
| THE BIRCHES, *Walter Prichard Eaton* | 95 |
| CATKIN, *Author Unknown* | 96 |
| A DEWDROP, *Frank Dempster Sherman* | 96 |
| CRESCENT MOON, *Elizabeth Madox Roberts* | 97 |
| THE DANDELION, *Mrs. E. J. H. Goodfellow* | 97 |
| FROZEN MILK BOTTLES, *Olive Beaupré Miller* | 98 |
| THE DANDELION, *Author Unknown* | 98 |
| THE LITTLE PLANT, *Kate Louise Brown* | 99 |
| FIRST SNOW, *Marie Louise Allen* | 99 |
| RAIN, *Robert Louis Stevenson* | 100 |
| THE ICICLE, *Mrs. Henry Gordon Gale* | 100 |
| MILK IN WINTER, *Rhoda W. Bacmeister* | 101 |
| I WONDER, *Mrs. Schuyler Van Renssalaer* | 101 |
| THE MOON, *Eliza Lee Follen* | 102 |
| RAIN, *Helen Wing* | 103 |
| THE MITTEN SONG, *Marie Louise Allen* | 103 |
| THE MOON, *May Morgan* | 104 |
| MERRY SUNSHINE, *Anonymous* | 104 |
| RAINING, *Rhoda W. Bacmeister* | 105 |
| THE TRAGEDY, *Anne Cooper* | 106 |
| SNOWFLAKES, *Mary Mapes Dodge* | 107 |
| SNOWFLAKES, *Elizabeth L. Cleveland* | 108 |
| RAINDROPS, *Isla Paschal Richardson* | 109 |
| ICE, *Dorothy Aldis* | 109 |

|  | Page |
|---|---|
| THE SNOWMAN, *Frances Frost* | 110 |
| SNOW, *Alice Wilkins* | 110 |
| WISE JOHNNY, *Edwina Fallis* | 111 |
| SNOWSTORM, *Rhoda W. Bacmeister* | 111 |
| RAIN IN THE NIGHT, *Amelia Josephine Burr* | 112 |
| WHEN BLUE SKY SMILES, *Olive Beaupré Miller* | 113 |
| MOON, SO ROUND AND YELLOW, *Matthias Barr* | 113 |
| JACK FROST, *Author Unknown* | 114 |
| THE RUNAWAY BROOK, *Eliza Lee Follen* | 114 |
| PUSSY WILLOW, *Kate L. Brown* | 115 |
| DANDELIONS, *Marietta W. Brewster* | 116 |
| TWINKLE, TWINKLE, LITTLE STAR, *Jane and Anne Taylor* | 116 |
| CLOUDS, *Author Unknown* | 117 |
| UNDER THE GROUND, *Rhoda W. Bacmeister* | 118 |
| THE PLAYING LEAVES, *Ora Clayton Moore* | 118 |
| MAY MORNING, *Marjorie Barrows* | 119 |
| THE WHITE WINDOW, *James Stephens* | 120 |
| WHERE DO ALL THE DAISIES GO?, *Anonymous* | 120 |

## PEOPLE

|  |  |
|---|---|
| TO BABY, *Kate Greenaway* | 125 |
| SLEEP, BABY, SLEEP, *Old Lullaby from the German* | 125 |
| PATRICK GOES TO SCHOOL, *Alicia Aspinwall* | 126 |
| MOTHER, *Rose Fyleman* | 127 |
| MRS. BROWN, *Rose Fyleman* | 128 |
| MY POLICEMAN, *Rose Fyleman* | 129 |

## RELIGIOUS POETRY

|  |  |
|---|---|
| BLESSING OVER FOOD, *H. N. Bialik* | 133 |
| A CHILD'S GRACE, *Author Unknown* | 133 |

|  | Page |
|---|---|
| Evening Hymn, *Anonymous* | 134 |

## SPECIAL DAYS

| | |
|---|---|
| A Halloween Meeting, *George O. Butler* | 137 |
| Was She a Witch, *Laura Elizabeth Richards* | 137 |
| Why Do the Bells of Christmas Ring?, *Eugene Field* | 138 |
| My Valentine, *Mary Catherine Parsons* | 138 |
| The Secret, *Helen Cowles Le Cron* | 139 |
| Riddle: What Am I?, *Dorothy Aldis* | 140 |
| When Santa Claus Comes, *Author Unknown* | 140 |
| Bundles, *John Farrar* | 141 |
| Meeting the Easter Bunny, *Rowena Bastian Bennett* | 141 |
| Birthdays, *Marchette Gaylord Chute* | 142 |

## TRANSPORTATION

| | |
|---|---|
| Funny the Way Different Cars Start, *Dorothy Baruch* | 147 |
| Engine, *James S. Tippett* | 148 |
| Stop—Go, *Dorothy Baruch* | 148 |

## WEE FOLKS AND MAGIC

| | |
|---|---|
| Fairies, *Hilda Conkling* | 153 |
| Fairies, *Marchette Gaylord Chute* | 153 |
| Fairy Aeroplanes, *Annie Blackwell Payne* | 154 |
| The Fairy Book, *Abbie Farwell Brown* | 154 |
| The Little Elf, *John Kendrick Bangs* | 156 |
| Fairy Shoes, *Annette Wynne* | 156 |
| Ring-A-Ring, *Kate Greenaway* | 157 |
| Please, *Rose Fyleman* | 158 |
| The Rainbow Fairies, *Lizzie M. Hadley* | 159 |
| Snow Fairies, *Isla Paschal Richardson* | 160 |

## Something About This Book

To the multitude of teachers who endeavor to so vitalize their instruction that learning is a joyous experience, this book is dedicated.

That choral reading is one of the channels through which just such teaching can be achieved is attested by Lucille A. Meltzer, of the Central School, Des Plaines, Illinois. In an article entitled "Ten Minutes a Day," in the December, 1946, issue of *Illinois Education,* Miss Meltzer says, in part, "I credit the children's love of poetry to the ten minutes a day we spend on choral reading. . . . The children really love this period. . . . Many tell how they always say them (i.e. the poems) after they are in bed and the light is out before they go to sleep."

In support of that testimony, a practical application of the principles and materials set forth in this volume was made with the assistance of a number of regular classroom teachers, representatives of city, village, and one- and two-room rural schools, from nearly every grade. Some weeks after the materials were given out, a visit was made to the schools of each of the teachers taking part in the project, to observe just how the activity was progressing. The evidence thus obtained of the educational value of *this kind of choral reading* as an aid in teaching the appreciation of poetry—even in the one-room school with only six pupils, and by teachers without any formal instruction or previous experience—gave substantial support to the conviction of the authors that teachers, generally, will find this book a treasury of useful materials.

Furthermore, in making the final selection of poems to be included, a considerable proportion of those appearing were first tried out in the classroom. The degree of enthusiasm with which each particular number was received by the pupils, and the ease with which it could be directed or taught determined whether or not it should be included. It seems certain that such "laboratory tested" principles and abundant materials will provide enjoyment and delight for the teacher and for the pupil.

## A Word About Choral Reading

Choral reading is as old as poetry itself. Together with the dance it furnished one of the earliest forms of artistic expression, running through the festivals and religious rites of primitive peoples, and antedating the theatre in the presentation of dramatic ideas. Its use for ritualistic purposes persists today in congregational reading of psalms and other liturgical literature in church worship.

The introduction into the schools of the United States of choral reading of prose and poetry for entertainment has come within the last twenty-five years. As a direct result, the activity has become so generally popular that verse choirs have sprung up, even within adult groups throughout the country, until there is scarcely a town of any size anywhere but can offer to its people this form of artistic recital on the programs of its public assemblies and other meetings which contribute to the cultural life of the community.

The primary purpose of this book is to make a delightful experience out of reading aloud *together* in school. At the same time, as a by-product, is bound to come a considerable contribution to the appreciation of poetry for the boys and girls who participate. Such appreciation will not arise predominantly from the usual inherent values of the literature itself, though that valuable factor has not been overlooked in making the selections for publication. It will come to the pupil through the sheer delight of joining with his schoolmates in expressing aloud the moods, rhythms, and community of ideas as they grow out of what constitutes a unique social experience.

In this approach, which the authors claim is new, the pleasure derived from choral reading does not differ essentially from the personal enjoyment which almost anyone feels when singing or playing a musical instrument in concert with others, whether or not there is an audience present, or the participants members of a formal musical organization. Furthermore, the particular choral arrangement for each selection in this book is designed to ensure, so far as possible, that the reading aloud together may be done, primarily, for the good fun in it.

## Procedures

In order to avoid the necessity for technical skill, which numbers of teachers using this work may feel they do not have, little attempt is made to classify or group the voices into light, medium, or dark. For the expression of various moods, somber to gay, the practical expedient is recommended of speaking in a lower or higher key, very much as everyone does when he "feels that way" in everyday life.

Likewise, the use of costumes, properties, or even special standing arrangements are not necessary to the effectiveness of the materials used in this book. For our present purposes the children may stand or sit in their regular places, at the discretion of the teacher, and read, under her direction, almost as spontaneously as they might break into singing "Happy Birthday to You," when it is announced that some one pupil has turned another year. It might be emphasized again, briefly, that the methods here are based on the principle of *participation* rather than on technical details or vocal effectiveness. Nevertheless, careful observation of the special arrangement of any selection in the book will reveal that some degree of this same vocal effectiveness has been attained frequently through solo and grouping devices which do not depend for their usefulness on the quality of voices nor the precise arrangement of parts or pupils. The following selection by Rachel Field is illustrative.

### THE LITTLE ROSE TREE

*All*
Every rose on the little tree
*Solo 1*
Is making a little face at me!
*Boys*
Some look surprised when I pass by,
*Girls*           *All*
And others droop—but they are shy.
*Duet*
These two whose heads together press

*Solo 2*
Tell secrets I could never guess.
*Boys*
Some have their heads thrown back to sing,
*Girls*
And all the buds are listening.
*Solo 3*
I wonder if the gardener knows,
*All*
Or if he calls each just a rose?

From *Pointed People*, by Rachel Field. Reprinted by permission of The Macmillan Company, publishers.

It should not be inferred from what has been said that special arrangement for effects is entirely sacrificed to schoolroom convenience. Rather, schoolroom convenience, from time to time, is made to contribute directly to the effectiveness of what is being read.

## Special Devices

Special instructions supporting the choral reading arrangements in this work are relatively few. Included are solos, duets, an occasional trio, quartet, quintet, pupils by rows, alternate reading by boys and girls, and one or two others.

It will be observed that all printed instructions accompanying the lines to be read appear, as a copyrighted convenience, in small type directly over the parts thus directed. This device, new to choral reading materials, makes it possible to see the words of the verse and the instruction for the reading at one and the same time. *It should be noted that the specific direction given in each instance is intended to prevail until a change is indicated by the next following suggestion.*

## The Solo

The solo device serves two specific purposes. First, it provides for the first personal pronoun, or what would ordinarily be understood to be the speaker himself. The following selection by Aileen Fisher furnishes an example.

## A COFFEEPOT FACE

### Aileen Fisher

*Solo*
I saw my face in the coffeepot.
*All*
Imagine, a coffeepot face!
*Solo*
My cheeks were big and my nose was *not,*
*All*
And my mouth was everyplace.

Reprinted by permission of *Child Life.*

Secondly, the solo is used to call attention to each of several different factors: (1) the meaning of a particular line, (2) the abrupt introduction of a new thought, (3) the expression of a subdued word, (4) phrase, (5) or sentence, (6) deep feeling, (7) and mock-seriousness. In addition to all these, it offers (8) the best possible means to give a number of different individual pupils an opportunity to participate in an important function of the reading. Occasionally the whole reading may be enhanced when (9) the teacher participates as a solo voice.

At least one example of each of the preceding items appears in the following selections. The appropriate number stands opposite the illustrative line.

(1) The Meaning of a Particular Line

### FAIRIES

#### Marchette Gaylord Chute

*Solo 1*
(1) You can't see fairies unless you're good,
*All*
That's what nurse said to me.
*Girls*
They live in the smoke or the chimney,
*Boys*
Or down in the roots of a tree;
*Girls*
They brush their wings on a tulip,

*Boys*
Or hide behind a pea.
*All*
But you can't see fairies unless you're good,
*Solo 2*
(1) So they aren't much use to me.


(2) The Abrupt Introduction of a New Thought

## MY DOG

### Marchette Gaylord Chute

*Boys*
He always wants to be going
Where he isn't supposed to go.
*Girls*
He tracks up the house when it's snowing—
*Solo*
(2) Oh, puppy, I love you so!

*My Dog* and *Fairies*, both by Marchette Gaylord Chute, are reprinted from *Rhymes About Ourselves*, by permission of The Macmillan Company, publishers.


(3) The Expression of a Subdued Word

## "SH"

### James S. Tippett

*Boy   Boys*
(3) "Sh!" says father,
*Girl   Girls*
(3) "Sh!" says mother.
*All*
"Can't you play a quiet game
Of some kind or other?"

From *I Live in the City*, by James S. Tippett. Copyright, 1927, by Harper and Brothers.

The following selection illustrates (8) as well as (4).

(4) Phrase (8) Different Individual Pupils

## SOME ONE

### Walter de la Mare

*Girl*
Someone came knocking
*Boy*
At my wee, small door;
*Boys*
Someone came knocking,
*Girls    Boys    All*
I'm sure—sure—sure!
*Solo 1*
I listened, I opened,
I looked to left and right,
*All*
But naught there was a-stirring
*Solo 2*
In the still dark night;
*Girls*
Only the busy beetle
*Solo 3*
Tap-tapping in the wall,
*Boys*
Only from the forest
*Solo 4*
The screech owl's call,
*Solo 5*
Only the cricket whistling
*Girls*
While the dewdrops fall,
*All*
So I know not who came knocking
*Boys    Girls    Solo 6*
At all, at all, at all.

(4)

From *Peacock Pie*, included in *Collected Poems*, by Walter de la Mare. Copyright, 1920, by Henry Holt and Company.

(5) Sentence

## SLEEP, BABY, SLEEP
### Old Lullaby

(5)
*Solo*
Sleep, baby, sleep!
*Boys*
Thy father watches the sheep.
*Girls*
Thy mother is shaking the dreamland tree,
*All*
And down falls a little dream for thee.
*Solo*
Sleep, baby, sleep!

(6) Deep Feeling

## BLESSING OVER FOOD
### H. N. Bialik

(6)
*All*
Blest be God
*Solo*
Who did create
*Girls*
Porridge with milk,
*Boys*
A whole full plate;
*All*
And after porridge
Also an orange.

From *Far Over the Sea,* by H. N. Bialik. Reprinted by permission of the Union of American Hebrew Congregations.

(7) Mock-seriousness

## ALAS! ALACK!
### Walter de la Mare

*Girl    Boy*
Ann, Ann!
*All*
Come! quick as you can!

8

*Row 1*
There's a fish that talks
*All*
In the frying pan.
*Row 2*
Out of the fat,
*Row 3*
As clear as glass,
*Row 4*
He put up his mouth
*Row 5*  *Solo 1*
(7)    And moaned, "Alas!"
*Row 6*
Oh, most mournful,
*Solo 1*
(7)    "Alas, alack!"
*Boys*
Then turned to his sizzling
*Solo 2*
(7)    And sank him back.

From *Peacock Pie*, included in *Collected Poems*, by Walter de la Mare. Copyright, 1920, by Henry Holt and Company.

(9) Teacher Participates

## WHAT ROBIN TOLD

### George Cooper

*Teacher*
(9)    How do robins build their nest?
*All*
Robin Redbreast told me.
*Row 1*
First a wisp of yellow hay
In a pretty round they lay;
*Row 2*
Then some shreds of downy floss,
*Row 3*
Feathers, too, and bits of moss,

9

*Row 4*
Woven with a sweet, sweet song,
This way, that way, and across;
*All*
That's what Robin told me.

It should be pointed out that where it is desirable to hear either a boy's or a girl's voice in a solo part, the corresponding instruction is given. If it makes no particular difference to the desired purpose who speaks the word or line, the term "Solo 1," "Solo 2," "Solo 3," etc., is used.

## Grouping

The duet, trio, quartet, or quintet is used where it is obvious from the accompanying lines or the meanings expressed that two, three, four, or five persons are involved.

Examples:

### Duet

*Solo*　　　　　　*Girls*
Once upon a time, in a wee little house,
*Duet*
Lived a funny old man and his wife;—

### Trio

*Girls*　　　　　　*Boys*
He called for his pipe, he called for his bowl,
*Trio*
And he called for his fiddlers three.

### Quartet

*Quartet*　　　　　　*Boys*
Four little monkeys sitting in a tree;
*All*　　　　　　*Girls*
Heads down, tails down, dreary as can be—

### Quintet

*Quintet*　　　　　　*All*
Five little monkeys swinging from a tree;
*Boys*　　　　　　*All*
Teasing Uncle Crocodile, merry as can be.

To express specific items in the progress of a selection, the speaking is arranged by rows, generally, throughout the book. It may be observed that sometimes the rows are paired, so as to include all the pupils in the room in the activity before the poem is completed. Six rows have been selected arbitrarily as the most common to schoolrooms, though it might as often be five or three. It is easy for a teacher to change the prescribed arrangement where the instruction indicated does not fit the seating plan for her room. Movable seats, of course, admit of any kind of seating arrangement desired.

Example:

## THE SONG OF THE ROBIN

### Beatrice Bergquist

*Row 1*
The cows low in the pasture on the hill,
*Row 2*
The bluebird sings building a nest,
*Row 3*
The water is singing down by the mill—
*All*
But the robin's song is the best!

*Row 4*
The squirrels are chattering in the trees,
*Row 5*
The wind is blowing toward the west,
*Row 6*
Around the flowers are humming bees—
*All*
But the robin's song is the best.

*Rows 1 and 2*
The dogwood trees are blossoming white,
*Rows 3 and 4*
The plough horse is neighing for rest,
*Rows 5 and 6*
The song sparrow is singing with all his might—
*All*
But the robin's song is the best.

Reprinted by permission of Gerda C. Bergquist.

## Girls and Boys

So far as there is any choice in passing the arrangement back and forth between boys and girls, an attempt has been made to assign the lines so that the traditionally diminutive, dainty, or reserved girls express the lines that are in minor key, or more or less subdued mood, while the boys contribute their supposed customary vigor and aggressiveness. An example follows.

### EXTREMES
#### James Whitcomb Riley

*Boys*
A little boy once played so loud
That the thunder, up in a thunder cloud
*Boy*
Said, "Since *I* can't be heard, why, then
*Boys*
I'll never, never thunder again!"

*Girls*
And a little girl once kept so still
That she heard a fly on the window sill
Whisper and say to a lady bird,—
*Girl*
"She's the stillest child I ever heard."

From *Book of Joyous Children*, by James Whitcomb Riley, copyright, 1902, 1930. Used by special permission of the publishers, The Bobbs-Merrill Company.

### Aid to Appreciation

Before proceeding with the choral reading of any selection, pupils should understand it—its meaning, mood, and movement. To this end, each number to be used should first be read aloud to the boys and girls by the teacher with the best interpretation she can bring to it. Frequently she can get some very good aids to her own reading if she will ask her pupils what particular words, phrases, or lines mean to them.

The choral arrangements appearing in this book are by no means the only possible, or desirable, ones. Any teacher may frequently find an original way of assigning parts, or draw suggestions from the pupils, which will fit the particular number better, for her purposes, than that suggested by the authors. The chief claim to the effectiveness of the printed instructions accompanying each selection is the convenience of having them ready at hand, and that they are practical, pleasurable, and educationally stimulating to children in the elementary schools.

## How to Start

As has been stated earlier, this volume is intended as a guide for the teacher in developing the choral speaking of poetry with which the children are familiar, as well as that which is new. In using verses already known, the teacher merely suggests the speaking of various lines by individual pupils or by groups, either from the arrangement appearing in the book, or by making one of her own choice.

For new material, memorization is easily accomplished in kindergarten and first grade where children have not yet learned to read, by speaking or reading any selection for them a number of times. Thus it is that the teacher may gradually familiarize her pupils with a large variety of verses from the book by frequently reading them aloud. As interest is shown in any particular number she may say to her class, "You may speak the poem with me." At first, perhaps, they will know only an occasional phrase or line, but by joining together with the teacher they will soon learn the entire piece. When memorizing has been accomplished, individual pupils may be chosen from volunteers to speak the solo lines, while the others participate in the group arrangement.

*Since it is not the purpose of this work to exploit special talents,* the choice of particular pupils will be varied, so that each child may experience, at one time or another, the pleasure which comes from speaking a solo, or by participating with the group in a way that produces within the speaker himself the special aesthetic response which is in keeping with the meaning and mood of the poem.

If the procedures used at any time demand too much of conscious effort, either on the part of the teacher or the pupils, it will defeat the very purpose of this particular type of choral reading. It is hoped that you will ever bear in mind that the sole aim of this book is to make the speaking together of poetry a delightful schoolroom experience.

# NURSERY RHYMES

## BAA, BAA, BLACK SHEEP

*Solo 1*
Baa, baa, black sheep,
*All*
Have you any wool?
*Solo 2*
Yes, sir, yes, sir,
Three bags full:
*Boy*
One for the master,
*Girl*
One for the dame,
*Girls*
But none for the little boy
*All*
Who cries in the lane.


## HICKORY DICKORY DOCK

*Girls*
Hickory, dickory, dock,
*All*
The mouse ran up the clock;
*Solo*
The clock struck One,
*Boys*
The mouse ran down,
*All*
Hickory, dickory, dock.


## A FARMER WENT RIDING

### Old Folk Rhyme

*Girls*
A farmer went riding upon his gray mare,
*Boys*           *Boy 1*
Bumpety, bumpety, bump!
*Girl 1*           *All*
With his daughter behind him, so rosy and fair,
*Boys*           *Boy 2*
Lumpety, lumpety, lump!

*Girl 2      Boy 3    All*
A raven cried "croak"! and they all tumbled down,
*Boys              Boy 4*
Bumpety, bumpety, bump!
*Girls*
The mare broke her knees and the farmer his crown,
*All              Boy 5*
Lumpety, lumpety, lump!

*Boys*
The mischievous raven flew laughing away,
*Girls             Girl 3*
Bumpety, bumpety, bump!
*Boys*
And vowed he would serve them the same the next day,
*Girls      Boys     All*
Humpety, humpety, hump.


## GOOSIE GANDER

*Girls*
Goosie, Goosie, Gander,
*Solo 1*
Whither did you wander?
*Boys      Girls*
Up stairs and down stairs
*All*
And in my lady's chamber.
*Solo 2*
There I met an old man,
*All*
Who would not say his prayers;
*Solo 3*
I took him by the left leg,
*All*
And threw him down the stairs.

## HEY DIDDLE DIDDLE

*All*
Hey, diddle, diddle,
*Girls*
The cat and the fiddle,
*Boys*
The cow jumped over the moon;
*Solo 1*
The little dog laughed
To see such sport,
*All*
And the dish ran away with the spoon.

## HUMPTY DUMPTY

*Girls*
Humpty Dumpty sat on a wall;
*Boys*
Humpty Dumpty had a great fall;
*Girls*
All the King's horses
*Boys*
And all the King's men
*All*
Couldn't put Humpty together again.

## I HAD A LITTLE PONY

*Solo 1*
I had a little pony,
I called him Dapple Gray,
I lent him to a lady
*All*
To ride a mile away.
*Girls*        *Boys*
She whipped him, she lashed him,
*All*
She rode him through the mire,
*Solo 1*
I would not lend my pony now,
*All*
For all the lady's hire.

## JACK AND JILL

*Boy   Girl*
Jack and Jill
*Duet*
Went up the hill
*All*
To fetch a pail of water;
*Girls*
Jack fell down
*Boys*
And broke his crown,
*All*
And Jill came tumbling after.

*Solo*
Up Jack got
*Girls*
And home did trot
*All*
As fast as he could caper;
*Boys*
He went to bed to mend his head,
*All*
With vinegar and brown paper.

## ONE, TWO, BUCKLE MY SHOE

*Girls Boys Solo 1*
One, two, buckle my shoe,
*Girls   Boys Solo 2*
Three, four, shut the door,
*Girls Boys Solo 3*
Five, six, pick up sticks,
*Girls   Boys   Solo 4*
Seven, eight, lay them straight,
*Girls Boys All*
Nine, ten, a big fat hen.

## LITTLE BO-PEEP

*Solo        Girls*
Little Bo-Peep has lost her sheep,
*Boys*
And can't tell where to find them;
*Girls        Boys*
Leave them alone, and they'll come home,
*All*
Bringing their tails behind them.

*Girls*
Little Bo-Peep fell fast asleep,
*Boys*
And dreamt she heard them bleating;
*Girls        Boys*
But when she awoke, she found it a joke,
*All*
For they were still a-fleeting.

*Girls*
Then up she took her little crook,
*Boys*
Determined for to find them;
*Boy*
She found them indeed
*Girl*
But it made her heart bleed,
*All*
For they'd left their tails behind them.

## LITTLE BOY BLUE

*Solo 1        All*
Little Boy Blue, come blow your horn;
*Girls*
The sheep's in the meadow,
*Boys*
The cow's in the corn.
*Solo 2*
Where's the little boy
That looks after the sheep?

    *Boys*                   *Girls*
He's under the haycock, fast asleep.
*Solo 2*           *Solo 3*
Will you wake him? No, not I;
       *All*
For if I do, he'll be sure to cry.

## LITTLE JACK HORNER

    *Solo 1*
Little Jack Horner
*Girls*
Sat in a corner,
*Boys*
Eating a Christmas pie;
*Girls*
He put in his thumb,
*Boys*
And pulled out a plum,
And said,
*Solo 2*
"What a good boy am I."

## LITTLE MISS MUFFET

*Girls*
Little Miss Muffet
*Boys*
Sat on a tuffet
*All*
Eating of curds and whey;
*Boys*
There came a big Spider
*Girls*
And sat down beside her,
*All*
And frightened Miss Muffet away.

## MISTRESS MARY

*Girls*
"Mistress Mary
*Boys*
Quite contrary
*All*
How does your garden grow?"
*Solo 1*
"With silver bells
*Solo 2*
And cockle shells,
*Girls*
And pretty maids, all in a row."


## LUCY LOCKET

*Solo 1*
Lucy Locket lost her pocket;
*Solo 2*
Kitty Fisher found it;
*All*
But not a penny was inside,
*Solo 3*
And only a binding round it.


## TOM, TOM, THE PIPER'S SON

*Solo 1*
Tom, Tom, the Piper's son,
*All*
Stole a pig and away he run.
*Boys*          *Girls*
The pig was eat and Tom was beat,
*All*
Which sent him howling down the street.

# RIDE-A-COCK HORSE

*Boys*
Ride-a-cock horse to Banbury Cross,
*Girls*
To see a fine lady upon a white horse;
*Boys*  *Girls*
Rings on her fingers and bells on her toes,
*All*
She shall have music where ever she goes.

## MARY HAD A LITTLE LAMB

*Solo 1*
Mary had a little lamb,
*Girls*
Its fleece was white as snow;
*All*
And everywhere that Mary went,
The lamb was sure to go.

*Boys*
He followed her to school one day,
*Solo 2*
Which was against the rule;
*All*
It made the children laugh and play
To see a lamb at school.

*Solo 3*
And so the teacher turned him out,
*Girls*
But still he lingered near,
*All*
And waited patiently about
Till Mary did appear.

*Solo 4*
Then, he ran to her, and laid
His head upon her arm,
*Solo 5*
As if he said, "I'm not afraid—
You'll keep me from all harm."

*All*
"What makes the lamb love Mary so?"
The eager children cry.
*Solo 6*
"Oh Mary loves the lamb, you know,"
*All*
The teacher did reply.

*Girls*
And you each gentle animal
In confidence may bind,
*Boys*
And make them follow at your will,
*All*
If you are only kind.

## MIX A PANCAKE

*Boys*
Mix a pancake,
*Girls*
Stir a pancake,
*All*
Pop it in the pan;
*Girls*
Fry the pancake,
*Boys*
Toss the pancake,
*All*
Catch it if you can.

## DING DONG BELL

*Solo 1*
Ding, dong, bell;
*All*
Pussy's in the well.
*Solo 2*
Who put her in?
*All*
Little Johnny Green.

*Solo 3*
Who pulled her out?
*All*
Big Johnny Stout.
*Girls*
What a naughty boy was that
To drown poor Pussy-cat,
*Boys*
She never did him any harm,
*All*
She killed the mice in his father's barn.


## OLD KING COLE

*Solo 1*
Old King Cole
*Girls*
Was a merry old soul,
*Boys*
And a merry old soul was he;
*Girls*
He called for his pipe,
*Boys*
And he called for his bowl,
*Trio*
And he called for his fiddlers three.
*Boys*
Every fiddler he had a fine fiddle,
*Girls*
And a very fine fiddle had he;
*Trio*
"Twee tweedle dee, tweedle dee," went the fiddlers.
*All*
Oh, there's none so rare,
As can compare
With King Cole and his fiddlers three.

## SING A SONG OF SIXPENCE

*All*
Sing a song of sixpence,
A pocket full of rye,
*Row 1*
Four-and-twenty blackbirds
*All*
Baked in a pie;
*Row 2*
When the pie was opened,
*Row 3*
The birds began to sing;
*All*
Wasn't that a dainty dish
To set before the king?

*Boys*
The king was in the counting-house
Counting out his money;
*Girls*
The queen was in the parlor
Eating bread and honey;
*Solo 1*
The maid was in the garden
*Row 4*
Hanging out the clothes,
*Solo 2*
Down came a blackbird,
*All*
And snapped off her nose.

## SOME LITTLE MICE

*All*
Some little mice sat in a barn to spin,
*Girls*          *Boys*
Pussy came by, and popped her head in.
*Solo*
"Shall I come in and cut your threads off?"
*Girls*          *All*
"Oh, no, kind Pussy, you may snap our heads off."

27

## PEASE PORRIDGE HOT

*Girls*
Pease porridge hot,
*Boys*
Pease porridge cold,
*All*
Pease porridge in the pot,
Nine days old.
*Girls*
Some like it hot,
*Boys*
Some like it cold,
*All*
But all like it in the pot,
Nine days old.


## THERE WAS A CROOKED MAN

*Row 1*
There was a crooked man,
*Row 2*
And he walked a crooked mile,
*Row 3*
He found a crooked sixpence
*All*
Against a crooked stile;
*Row 4*
He bought a crooked cat,
*Row 5*
Which caught a crooked mouse,
*All*
And they all lived together
In a little crooked house.

# WHEN I WAS A LITTLE BOY
## Old English Rhyme

*Boy 1*
When I was a little boy,
I lived by myself;
And all the bread and cheese I got
I put upon a shelf.
*All*
The rats and the mice—
They led me such a life
*Boy 2*
I had to go to London
To get myself a wife.

*Boys*
The streets were so bad,
*Girls*
And the roads were so narrow,
*Boy 3*
I had to bring her home
*Girls*
In a little wheelbarrow.
*Boys*
The wheelbarrow broke,
*Boy 4*
And my wife had a fall.
*All*
Down tumbled wheelbarrow,
Little wife and all.

## PAT-A-CAKE

*All*
Pat-a-cake, pat-a-cake, baker's man!
Make me a cake as fast as you can.
*Solo 1  Solo 2*
Pat it, and prick it,
*Solo 3*
And mark it with T,
*All*
And bake in the oven
For Baby and me.

# CHILDHOOD MYSTERY AND EXPERIENCE

# THE CUPBOARD

### Walter de la Mare

*Solo 1*
I know a little cupboard,
*All*
With a teeny tiny key,
And there's a jar of Lollypops
*Solo 1   S. 2   S. 3*
For me, me, me.

*Girls*
It has a little shelf, up high,
*Boys*
As dark as dark can be,
*All*
And there's a dish of Banbury Cakes
*Solo 4   S. 5   S. 6*
For me, me, me.

*Solo 1*
I have a small fat grandmother,
*All*
With a very slippery knee,
*Girls*
And she's keeper of the Cupboard,
*Solo 7         Girls Boys*
With the key, key, key.

*Solo 1*
And when I'm very good, you know,
*All*
As good as good can be,
*Boys                    Girls*
There's Banbury Cakes, and Lollypops
*Solo 8     S. 9   S. 10*
For me, me, me.

From *Peacock Pie*, included in *Collected Poems*, by Walter de la Mare. Copyright, 1920, by Henry Holt and Company.

# BRIDGES

### Rhoda W. Bacmeister

*Solo 1*
I like to look for bridges
Everywhere I go,
*Boys*
Where the cars go over
With water down below.

*Girls*
Standing by the railings
*Solo 2*
I watch the water slide
Smoothly under to the dark,
*All*
And out the other side.

From *Stories to Begin On,* by Rhoda W. Bacmeister, published and copyright by E. P. Dutton & Company, Inc., New York. 1929, Dutton; 1940, Dutton, respectively.


# ABOUT BUTTONS

### Dorothy Aldis

*Solo 1*
Every button has a door
*All*
Which opens wide to let him in;
*Girls*
But when he rolls upon the floor,
*Boys*
Because he's tired of where he's been
*Solo 2*
And we can't find him any more,
*All*
We use a pin.

From *Here, There and Everywhere,* by Dorothy Aldis. Copyright, 1927, 1928, by Dorothy Aldis. Courtesy of G. P. Putnam's Sons, New York.

# ECHO

### Author Unknown

*Solo 1*
I sometimes wonder where he lives,
*All*
This Echo that I never see.
*Girls*
I hear his voice now in the hedge,
*Boys*
Then down behind the willow tree.

*All*          *Solo 2*
And when I call, "Oh, please come out,"
*Solo 3*      *All*
"Come out," he always quick replies.
*Solo 2*      *All*
"Hello, hello," again I say;
*Solo 3*      *Girls*
"Hello, hello," he softly cries.

*All*
He must be jolly, Echo must,
*Boys*
For when I laugh, "Ho, ho, ho, ho,"
Like any other friendly boy,
           *Girls*
He answers me with "Ho, ho, ho."

*Solo 4*
I think perhaps he'd like to play;
I know some splendid things to do.
*All*
He must be lonely hiding there;
*Solo 5*      *All*
I wouldn't like it. Now, would you?

## EVERYBODY SAYS

### Dorothy Aldis

*All*
Everybody says
*Solo 1*
I look just like my mother,
*All*
Everybody says
*Solo 2*
I'm the image of Aunt Bee,
*All*
Everybody says
*Solo 3*
My nose is like my father's,
*Trio*
But I want to look like me.

From *Everything and Anything*, by Dorothy Aldis. Copyright, 1925, 1926, 1927, by Dorothy Aldis. Courtesy of G. P. Putnam's Sons, New York.

## GALOSHES

### Rhoda W. Bacmeister

*Solo 1*
Susie's galoshes
*Girls*
Make splishes and sploshes
*Boys*
And slooshes and sloshes,
*All*
As Susie steps slowly
Along in the slush.

*Girls*
They stamp and they tramp
On the ice and concrete,
*Boys*
They get stuck in the muck and the mud;
*Solo 2*
But Susie likes much best to hear

35

The slippery slush
*Boys*
As it slooshes and sloshes,
*Girls*
And splishes and sploshes,
*All*
All round her galoshes!

From *Stories to Begin On,* by Rhoda Bacmeister. Published and copyright by E. P. Dutton & Company, Inc., New York. 1929, Dutton; 1940, Dutton, respectively.

## GROWING UP

### Author Unknown

*All*
My birthday is coming tomorrow,
*Solo 1*
And then I'm going to be four;
*All*
And I'm getting so big that already
I can open the kitchen door;
*Solo 2*
I'm very much taller than Baby,
Though today I am still only three;
*Solo 3*
And I'm bigger than Bob-tail the puppy,
*All*
Who used to be bigger than me.

## HIDING

### Dorothy Aldis

*Solo 1*
I'm hiding, I'm hiding,
*All*
And no one knows where;
*Girls*                *Solo 1*
For all they can see is my
Toes and my hair.

36

*Boys*
And I just heard my father
Say to my mother——
*Solo 2*
"But, darling, he must be
Somewhere or other;

*Solo 3*
"Have you looked in the inkwell?"
*All*                *Solo 3*
And Mother said, "Where?"
*Solo 2*           *All*         *Solo 1*
"In the inkwell," said Father. But
I was not there.

*All*     *Solo 3*    *All*
Then, "Wait!" cried my Mother——
*Solo 3*
"I think that I see
                    *Solo 1*
Him under the carpet." But
It was not me.

*Solo 2*
"Inside the mirror's
A pretty good place,"
*Boys*                    *All*
Said Father and looked, but saw
Only his face.

*Solo 3*           *Girls*
"We've hunted," sighed Mother,
*Solo 3*
"As hard as we could
And I *am* so afraid that we've
Lost him for good."

*Solo 1*
Then I laughed out loud
And I wiggled my toes
*All*                *Solo 2*
And Father said, "Look, dear,
I wonder if those

37

Toes could be Benny's?
There are ten of them, see?"
*All*
And they *were* so surprised to find
*Solo 1*
Out it was me.

From *Everything and Anything*, by Dorothy Aldis. Copyright, 1925, 1926, 1927, by Dorothy Aldis. Courtesy of G. P. Putnam's Sons, New York.

### MERRY-GO-ROUND

#### Dorothy W. Baruch

*Solo 1*
I climbed up on the merry-go-round,
*Girls*
And it went round and round.

*Solo 2*
I climbed up on a big brown horse,
*Boys*
And it went up and down.
*Girls*
Around and round and up and down,
*Boys*
Around and round and up and down.
*Solo 3*
I sat high up on a big brown horse
*Girls*
And rode around on the merry-go-round
*Boys*
And rode around on the merry-go-round
*Solo 4*
I rode around on the merry-go-round
*Boys*
Around
*Girls*
And round
*Solo 5*
And
Round.

Reprinted by special permission of Dorothy W. Baruch and by Harper & Brothers, publishers.

# ICY

### Rhoda W. Bacmeister

*Solo 1*
I slip and I slide
*Girls*
On the slippery ice;
*Solo 2*
I skid and I glide,—
*Girls*
Oh, isn't it nice
*Boys*
To lie on your tummy
And slither and skim
On the slick crust of snow
*All*
Where you skid as you swim?

From *Stories to Begin On*, by Rhoda Bacmeister. Published and copyright by E. P. Dutton & Company, Inc., New York. 1929, Dutton; 1940, Dutton, respectively.

# LULLABY

### Sarah Jane S. Harrington

*Solo 1*
Sleep, my little one, sleep,
*All*
For twinkling stars will light the way
To dreamland just a dream away—
*Solo 2*
So sleep, my baby, sleep—
*Boys    Girls    Solo 3*
Sleep, sleep, sleep.

*Solo 4*
Sleep, my little one, sleep,
*All*
For little clouds are sailing by
To find their cradles in the sky—
*Solo 5*
So, sleep, my baby, sleep—
*Boys    Girls    Solo 6*
Sleep, sleep, sleep.

*Solo 7*
Sleep, my little one, sleep,
*Boys*
The little birds no longer cheep,
*Girls*
But 'neath the mother wings they creep—
*Solo 8*
So sleep, my baby, sleep—
*Boys   Girls   Solo 9*
Sleep, sleep, sleep.

*Solo 10*
Sleep, my little one, sleep,
*Girls*
The silver moon is watching thee,
*All*
Her little beams have come to see
My baby going to sleep—
*Boys   Girls   Solo 11*
Sleep, sleep, sleep.

By special arrangement with Mildred P. Harrington, present holder of the copyright.

## FIVE YEARS OLD

### Marie Louise Allen

*All*
Please, everybody look at me!
*Solo 1*
Today, I'm five years old, you see!
*All*
And after this, I won't be four,
Not ever, ever, any more!
*Solo 2*
I won't be three—or two—or one,
*All*
For that was when I'd first begun.
*Solo 3*
Now I'll be five a while, and then
*All*
I'll soon be something else again!

From *A Pocketful of Rhymes*, by Marie Louise Allen. Copyright, 1939, by Harper and Brothers.

# MILKING TIME

### Elizabeth Madox Roberts

*All*
When supper time is almost come,
*Girls          Solo 1*
But not quite here, I cannot wait,
And so I take my china mug
*All*
And go down by the milking gate.

*Boys*
The cow is always eating shucks
And spilling off the little silk;
*Girls*
Her purple eyes are big and soft—
*All*
She always smells like milk.

*Solo 2*
And father takes my mug from me,
*All*
And then he makes the stream come out.
*Solo 3*
I see it going in my mug
*All*
And foaming all about.

*Boys*
And when it's piling very high,
*Girls*
And when some little streams commence
To run and drip along the sides,
*All*
He hands it to me through the fence.

From *Under the Tree*, by Elizabeth Madox Roberts. Copyright, 1922, by B. W. Huebsch. By permission of The Viking Press, Inc., New York.

# MUD

### Polly Chase Boyden

*Girls*
Mud is very nice to feel
*Boys*
All squishy-squash between the toes!
*Solo 1*
I'd rather wade in wiggly mud
*All*
Than smell a yellow rose.

*Solo 2*
Nobody else but the rosebush knows
*Girls*
How nice mud feels
*Boys*
Between the toes.

Courtesy, *Child Life*, Boston, Massachusetts.

# MY FUNNY UMBRELLA

### Alice Wilkins

*All*
Oh, isn't it fun—when the rain comes down?
*Solo 1*
I like to go walking way down in the town.
*Boys*
The wind blows in gusts with all of its might,
*Girls*
And makes my umbrella dance,—just like a kite.

*Solo 2*          *Solo 3*
It waves first to one side, and then back it flies—
*Solo 4*          *All*
To sail off without me, it certainly tries!
*Solo 5*
One day I had walked and was home—just about—
*All*
And my funny umbrella turned right inside out.

From *The Golden Flute* (The John Day Company), by Alice Hubbard and Adeline Babbitt. By permission of Miss Hubbard.

# MY SHADOW

## Robert Louis Stevenson

*Solo 1*
I have a little shadow that goes in and out with me,
*All*
And what can be the use of him is more than I can see.
*Solo 2*
He is very, very like me from his heels up to his head;
*All*
And I see him jump before me when I jump into my bed.

*Girls*
The funniest thing about him is the way he likes to grow——
*Boys*
Not at all like proper children, which is always very slow;
*Solo 3*
For he sometimes shoots up taller like an India-rubber ball,
*Solo 4*
And he sometimes gets so little that there's none of him at all.

*All*
He hasn't got a notion of how children ought to play,
*Solo 5*
And can only make a fool of me in every sort of way.
*Solo 6*
He stays so close beside me, he's a coward you can see;
*Solo 7*
I'd think shame to stick to nursie as that shadow sticks to me.

*All*
One morning, very early, before the sun was up,
*Solo 8*
I rose and found the shining dew on every buttercup;
*Solo 9*
But my lazy little shadow, like an errant sleepy head,
*Solo 10*          *All*
Had stayed at home beside me and was fast asleep in bed.

From *A Child's Garden of Verses*, by Robert Louis Stevenson. By permission of The Macmillan Company, publishers.

## MY ZIPPER SUIT

### Marie Louise Allen

*Solo 1*
My zipper suit is bunny brown——
*Girls            Boys*
The top zips up, the legs zip down.
*Solo 2*
I wear it every day.
*Solo 3*
My daddy brought it out from town.
*Girls     Boys*
Zip it up, and zip it down,
*All*
And hurry out to play!

From *A Pocketful of Rhymes*, by Marie Louise Allen. Copyright, 1939, by Harper & Brothers.


## MY KITE

### Barbara and Beatrice Brown

*Solo 1*
The busy wind is out today
*All*
A-blowing all the clouds away
*Boys*
And chasing butterflies and bees
*Girls*
And making music in the trees.
*Solo 2*
My kite it carries far and high
*All*
Till it is lost up in the sky.

Courtesy, The Christian Science Publishing Society, Boston, Massachusetts.

## NAUGHTY SOAP SONG

### Dorothy Aldis

*Solo 1*
Just when I'm ready to
Start on my ears,
*All*
That is the time that my
Soap disappears.

*Solo 2*
It jumps from my fingers and
*Girls*
Slithers and slides
Down to the end of the
Tub, where it hides.

*Boys*
And acts in a most diso-
Bedient way;
*All*
And that's why my soap's growing
Thinner each day!

From *Everything and Anything*, by Dorothy Aldis. Copyright, 1925, 1926, 1927, by Dorothy Aldis. Courtesy of G. P. Putnam's Sons, New York.


## NEW SHOES

### Alice Wilkins

*Boys*
I have new shoes in the fall-time
*Girls*
And new ones in the spring.
*Solo*
Whenever I wear my new shoes
*All*
I always have to sing!

From *The Golden Flute* (The John Day Company), by Alice Hubbard and Adeline Babbitt. By permission of Miss Hubbard.

# THE PARK

## James S. Tippett

*Solo 1*
I'm glad that I live near a park
*Girls*
For in the winter after dark
*Boys*
The park lights shine as bright and still
*All*
As dandelions on a hill.

From *I Live in the City*, by James S. Tippett. Copyright, 1927, by Harper and Brothers.

# SPRINKLING

## Dorothy Mason Pierce

*All*
Sometimes in the summer
When the day is hot
*Boys*
Daddy takes the garden hose
*Girls*
And finds a shady spot;
*Boys*
Then he calls me over,
*Girls*
Looks at my bare toes
*Solo*
And says, "Why, you need sprinkling,
You thirsty little rose!"

Used by special permission of the author.

## HAIR RIBBONS
### Author Unknown

*Solo 1*
I'm three years old and like to wear
A bow of ribbon on my hair.
*Girls              Boys*
Sometimes it's pink, sometimes it's blue;
*All*
I think it's pretty there, don't you?


## BOOTS, BOOTS, BOOTS
### Leroy F. Jackson

*Solo 1*
Buster's got a popper gun,
*Boys*
A reg'lar one that shoots,
*Solo 2*
And Teddy's got an engine
*Girls*
With a whistler that toots.

*Solo 3*
But I've got something finer yet—
*All*
A pair of rubber boots—
*Girls         Boys    All*
Oh, it's boots, boots, boots,
*Duet*
A pair of rubber boots!
*Solo 4*
I could walk from here to China
*All*
In a pair of rubber boots.

From *The Peter Patter Book,* by Leroy F. Jackson. Copyright, 1918, renewal copyright, 1946, by Rand McNally and Company, publishers.

## TROUBLES

### Dorothy Aldis

*All*                    *Solo 1*
Stockings are a trouble; so many times my toes
*Boys*
Try to climb in where a heel generally goes.

*All*                    *Solo 2*
And mittens are not easy, for lots of times my thumbs
*Girls*
Go wandering and crawling into other fingers' homes.

*All*                    *Solo 3*
But rubbers are the hardest because, it seems to me,
*Solo 4*              *All*
I always put one rubber where the other ought to be.

From *Here, There and Everywhere*, by Dorothy Aldis. Copyright, 1927, 1928, by Dorothy Aldis. Courtesy of G. P. Putnam's Sons, New York.


## ROCKING HORSE

### H. N. Bialik. Translated by Jessie Sampter

*Boys*
My rocking horse rocks and rocks,
*Girls*
And my head swims and swells,
*Solo 1*
It's I that's going round,
It's I and no one else!

*All*
Streets and houses are rushing!
*Boys*             *Girls*
Where's their end, their beginning?
*Solo 2*
Like a wheel in a wheel
*All*
Round and round they are spinning.

*Solo 3*
There, my trumpet goes flop,
*All*
There, it falls on its crown!
*Solo 4*
Hold me fast, or I too
*All*
Shall go tumbling down!

From *Far Over the Sea,* published by the Union of American Hebrew Congregations, and used with their permission.

## A POP CORN SONG

### Nancy Byrd Turner

*All*
Sing a song of pop corn
When the snowstorms rage;
*Boys*
Fifty little brown men
Put into a cage.
*Girls*
Shake them till they laugh and leap,
Crowding to the top,
*All*
Watch them burst their little coats
*Row 1   Row 2   Row 3*
Pop!!   Pop!!   Pop!!

*Solo 1*
Sing a song of pop corn
In the firelight;
*Girls*
Fifty little fairies
Robed in fleecy white.
*Boys*
Through the shining wires see
How they skip and prance
To the music of the flames;
*Row 4    Row 5    Row 6*
Dance!!  Dance!!  Dance!!

*All*
Sing a song of pop corn
*Solo 2*
Done the frolicking;
*Girls*
Fifty little fairies
Strung upon a string.
*Boys*
Cool and happy, hand in hand,
Sugar-spangled, fair;
*Solo 3*
Isn't that a necklace fit
For any child to wear?

From *St. Nicholas Magazine*. Used by permission of the author, and by D. Appleton-Century Company.

## SEE-SAW

### H. N. BIALIK. TRANSLATED BY JESSIE SAMPTER

*All*
See-saw, see-saw,
Fly and fall, fall and fly!
*Solo 1      Solo 2*
What is low and what is high?
*Solo 3   Duet*
Only I, just you and I.

*Duet*
We two are weighed
*Girls*
Are balanced even
*All*
On scales between
Earth and heaven.

From *Far Over the Sea*, published by the Union of American Hebrew Congregations, and used with their permission.

## SEESAW

### Evelyn Beyer

*Girls*
Up and down,
*Boys*
Up and down,
*Girls*
Seesaws pop
Up,
*Boys*
Seesaws drop
Down.

*Girls*
The down is a bump,
*Boys*
The up is a jump.
*Girls*
See-saw,
*Boys*
See-saw,
*All*
UP!

From *Another Here and Now Story Book*, edited by Lucy Sprague Mitchell, published and copyright by E. P. Dutton and Company, Inc., New York, and used by special permission of the publishers.


## THE SECRET

### Author Unknown

*All*        *Trio* *
We have a secret, just we three
*Solo 1*    *Solo 2 Solo 3*
The robin, and I, and the sweet cherry tree;
*All*         *Solo 2*
The bird told the tree, and the tree told me,
*All*         *Trio*
And nobody knows it but just us three.

* Solo parts may be taken by children in the trio.

*All*
But of course the robin knows it best,
                    *Solo 1*
Because he built the—— I sha'n't tell the rest;
*All*                *Solo 2*
And laid the four little—— something in it——
*Solo 3*
I'm afraid I shall tell it every minute.

*All*
But if the tree and the robin don't peep,
*Solo 2*
I'll try my best the secret to keep;
                    *All*
Though I know when the little birds fly about
Then the whole secret will be out.


## "SH"

### James S. Tippett

*Solo 1 Girls*
"Sh!" says mother,
*Solo 2 Boys*
"Sh!" says father.
*All*
"Running in the hall
Is a very great bother.

*Solo 3*
"Mrs. Grumpy Grundy,
*Boys*
Who lives down below,
*Solo 4*
Will come right up
*Girls*
First thing you know."

*Solo 5 Boys*
"Sh!" says father,
*Solo 6 Girls*
"Sh!" says mother.
*All*
"Can't you play a quiet game
Of some kind or other?"

From *I Live in the City,* by James S. Tippett. Copyright, 1927, by Harper and Brothers.

## SKYSCRAPERS

### Rachel Field

*Girls*
Do skyscrapers ever grow tired
*All*
Of holding themselves up high?
*Boys*
Do they ever shiver on frosty nights
*All*
With their tops against the sky?

*Row 1*
Do they feel lonely sometimes
*Girls*
Because they have grown so tall?
*Boys*
Do they ever wish they could lie right down
*All*
And never get up at all?

From *Pointed People,* by Rachel Field, published by The Macmillan Company, and used with their permission.

# SMELLS (JUNIOR)

### Christopher Morley

*Row 1*
My daddy smells like tobacco and books,
*Row 2*
Mother, like lavender and listerine;
*Row 3*
Uncle John carries a whiff of cigars,
*Row 4*
Nannie smells starchy and soapy and clean.

*Row 5*
Shandy, my dog, has a smell of his own
*Boy*
(When he's been out in the rain he smells most);
*Row 6*
But Katie, the cook, is more splendid than all——
*All*
She smells exactly like hot buttered toast.

From *The Rocking Horse,* copyright, 1919, 1946, by Christopher Morley, published by J. B. Lippincott Company.


# SOAP BUBBLES

### Author Unknown

*Boys*
Fill the pipe!
*Girls*
Gently blow;
*All*
Now you'll see
The bubbles grow!
*Boys*
Strong at first,
*Girls*
Then they burst,
*All*
Then they go to
Nothing, Oh!

## SNEEZING

### Marie Louise Allen

*Girls*
Air comes in tickly
Through my nose,
*Boys*
Then very quickly——
Out it goes:
*All*
Ahhh————CHOO!

*Solo*
With every sneeze
I have to do,
I make a breeze——
*Girls*                      *Boys*
Ahhh————CHOO!————Ahhh————CHOO!

From *A Pocketful of Rhymes*, by Marie Louise Allen. Copyright, 1939, by Harper and Brothers.


## SPINNING TOP

### Frank Dempster Sherman

*Solo*
When I spin round without a stop
*All*
And keep my balance like a top,
*Solo*
I find that soon the floor will swim
                 *All*
Before my eyes; and then, like him,
*Solo*
I lie all dizzy on the floor
*All*
Until I feel like spinning more.

Used by special permission of the author, and by Houghton Mifflin Company.

## HIPPITY HOP TO BED

### Leroy F. Jackson

*All*
O it's hippity hop to bed!
*Solo 1*
I'd rather sit up instead.
*Solo 2*
But when father says "must,"
*All*
There's nothing but just
Go hippity hop to bed.

Used by permission of the author.


## WHISTLE

### Author Unknown

*Solo 1*
I want to learn to whistle,
*All*
I've always wanted to;
*Solo 2*          *All*
I fix my mouth to do it, but
The whistle won't come through.

*Solo 3*
I think perhaps it's stuck, and so
I try it once again;
*All*
Can people swallow whistles,
*Solo 4*
Where is my whistle then?

## THE LITTLE DREAMER
### Old Rhyme

*Solo 1*
A little boy was dreaming,
Upon his mother's lap,
*Girls*
That the pins fell out of all the stars,
*Boys*
And the stars fell into his cap.

*Girls*
So, when his dream was over,
*Boys*
What did this little boy do?
*Solo 2*
Why, he went and looked inside his cap,
*All*
And found it was not true.


## WHO'S IN
### Elizabeth Fleming

*Boys*
"The door is shut fast
And everyone's out."
*Girls*
But people don't know
What they're talking about!

*Row 1*
Says the fly on the wall,
*Row 2*
And the flame on the coals,
*Row 3*
And the dog on his rug
*Row 4*
And the mice in their holes,

*Row 5*
And the kitten curled up,
*Row 6*
And the spiders that spin——
*Solo 1*
"What, everyone out?
*All*
Why, everyone's in!"

Used by special arrangement with the publishers, W. Collins Sons and Company, Ltd., London, England.

# LIVING THINGS

# BIRD'S NEST

### H. N. BIALIK. TRANSLATED BY JESSIE SAMPTER

*Boys*
Among the trees
Is a bird's nest,
*Girls*
And in the nest
Her three eggs rest.

*All*
And in each egg——
*Solo*
Hush, you'll be heard!——
*All*
There lies asleep
A tiny bird.

From *Far Over the Sea*, by H. N. Bialik. Published by the Union of American Hebrew Congregations, and used with their permission.

## THE CHICKENS

### ANONYMOUS

*Girls*
Said the first little chicken,
With a queer little squirm,
*Solo 1*
"I wish I could find
A fat little worm."

*Boys*
Said the next little chicken,
With an odd little shrug:
*Solo 2*
"I wish I could find
A fat little bug."

*Girls*
Said a third little chicken,
With a small sigh of grief:
*Solo 3*
"I wish I could find
A green little leaf!"

*Boys*
Said the fourth little chicken,
With a faint little moan:
*Solo 4*
"I wish I could find
A wee gravel stone."

*Solo 5*　　　　*Girls*
"Now, see here!" said the mother,
From the green garden patch,
*Solo 5*
"If you want any breakfast,
*All*
Just come here and scratch!"

## CRICKETS

### Helen Wing

*Solo 1*
What makes the crickets "crick" all night
*All*
And never stop to rest?
*Girls*
They must take naps in daytime
*Boys*
So at night they'll "crick" their best.
*Solo 2*
I wonder if they just take turns
And try to make it rhyme;
*Solo 3*
Or do a million crickets
*All*
Keep "cricking" all the time?

Used by special arrangement with the author.

## TRACKS

### John Farrar

*Solo*
I wonder where the rabbits go
*All*
Who leave their tracks across the snow;
*Solo*
For when I follow to their den
*All*
The tracks always start right out again.

From *Songs for Parents,* by John Farrar. Reprinted by arrangement with Yale University Press, publishers.


## LITTLE BUG

### Rhoda W. Bacmeister

*Solo 1*
A weeny little bug
*Girls*
Goes climbing up the grass,
*All*
What a lot of tiny little legs he has!

*Solo 2*
I can see his eyes,
*Boys*
Small and black and shiny.
*Solo 3*
I CAN'T THINK how it feels to be so tiny!

From *Stories to Begin On,* by Rhoda W. Bacmeister. Published and copyright by E. P. Dutton & Company, Inc., New York. 1929, Dutton; 1940, Dutton, respectively.

## THE DUCK
### EDITH KING

*Solo 1*
If I were in a tulip tub,
*All*
And it were my good luck
*Solo 2*
To have a wish, I'd choose to be
A lovely snow-white duck.

*Girls*
When she puts off into the pond,
*Solo 3*
And leaves me on the brink,
*Boys*
She wags her stumpy tail at me,
*All*
And gives a saucy wink,

*Row 1*
Which says as plain as words could say
*Solo 4*
I'm safe as safe can be,
Stay there, or you will drown yourself,
The pond was made for me.

*Row 2*
She goes a-sailing to and fro,
Just like a fishing boat,
*Row 3*
And steers and paddles, all herself,
And never wets her coat.

*Row 4*
Then in the water, upside down,
*Solo 5*
I've often seen her stand,
More neatly than the little boys
Who do it on the land.

*Row 6*
And, best of all, her children are
The ducklings, bright as gold,
Who swim about the pond with her,
*All*
And do as they are told.

From *Fifty New Poems for Children*, reprinted by special permission of Basil Blackwell and Mott, Ltd., Oxford, England.


## FAMILIAR FRIENDS

### James S. Tippett

*Row 1      Row 2      Row 3*
The horses, the pigs, and the chickens,
*Row 4      Row 5      Row 6*
The turkeys, the ducks, and the sheep!
*Solo 1*
I can see all my friends from the window
As soon as I waken from sleep.

*Row 1*
The cat on the fence is out walking.
*Row 2*
The geese have gone down for a swim.
*Row 3*
The pony comes trotting right up to the gate;
*Solo 2*
He knows I have candy for him.

*Row 4*
The cows in the pasture are switching
Their tails to keep off the flies.
*Solo 3                        All*
And the old mother dog has come out in the yard
        *Solo 4*
With five pups to give me a surprise.

From *I Spend the Summer*, by James S. Tippett. Copyright, 1930, by Harper and Brothers.

## FIREFLIES

### Grace Wilson Coplen

*All*
I like to chase the fireflies,
*Girls*
Chase them to and fro;
*Boys*
I like to watch them dart about,
*All*
Their little lamps aglow.

*Girls*
In the evening's twilight dim
*Solo 1*
I follow them about;
*Solo 2*
I often think I have one caught,
*All*
And then his light goes out.

*Solo 3*
I cannot tell just where he is
*Boys*
Until he winks, you see,
*Solo 4*
Then far away I see his light,
*All*
He's played a joke on me.

Used by special arrangement with The Parents' Institute, Inc., publishers.

## THE GOLDFISH

### Dorothy Aldis

*Solo 1*
My darling little goldfish
Hasn't any toes;
*Girls*
He swims around without a sound
*Boys*
And bumps his hungry nose.

*All*
He can't get out to play with me,
*Solo 2*
Nor I get in to him,
    *Solo 3*
Although I say: "Come out and play,"
*All*   *Solo 4*
And he: "Come in and swim."

From *Everything and Anything,* by Dorothy Aldis. Copyright, 1925, 1926, 1927, by Dorothy Aldis. Courtesy of G. P. Putnam's Sons, New York.

# GOOD MORNING

### Muriel Sipe

*Solo 1*
One day I saw a downy duck,
*All*
With feathers on his back;
*Solo 1*
I said, "Good morning, downy duck,"
*Solo 2*   *All*
And he said, "Quack, quack, quack."

*Solo 3*
One day I saw a timid mouse,
*Solo 4*
He was so shy and meek;
*Solo 3*
I said, "Good morning, timid mouse,"
*All*   *Solo 4*
And he said, "Squeak, squeak, squeak."

*Solo 5*
One day I saw a curly dog,
I met him with a bow;
I said, "Good morning, curly dog,"
*Solo 6*   *All*
And he said, "Bow-wow-wow."

*Solo 7*
One day I saw a scarlet bird,
*Solo 8*
He woke me from my sleep;
*Solo 9*
I said, "Good morning, scarlet bird,"
*All*      *Solo 10*
And he said, "Cheep, cheep, cheep."

Reprinted by special permission of the author.

## I LOVE LITTLE PUSSY

### Jane Taylor

*Solo 1*
I love little Pussy,
*Girls*
Her coat is so warm;
*Solo 2*
And if I don't hurt her
*Boys*
She'll do me no harm.
*Solo 3*
So I'll not pull her tail,
*All*
Nor drive her away,

*Solo 1*
But Pussy and I
Very gently will play;
*Solo 2*
She shall sit by my side,
And I'll give her some food;
*All*
And she'll love me because
I am gentle and good.

## THE HOUSE CAT

### Annette Wynne

*All*
The house cat sits
*Boys        Girls*
And smiles and sings.
*All*
He knows a lot of
*Solo*
Secret things.

From *For Days and Days,* by Annette Wynne. Copyright, 1919, by J. B. Lippincott Company, and reprinted with their permission.

## MRS. PECK-PIGEON

### Eleanor Farjeon

*All*
Mrs. Peck-Pigeon
Is picking for bread,
*Solo 1*
Bob-bob-bob
*Boys*
Goes her little round head.
*Girls*
Tame as a pussy-cat
In the street,
*Solo 2*
Step-step-step
Go her little red feet.
*Girls*
With her little red feet
*Boys*
And her little round head,
*All*
Mrs. Peck-Pigeon
Goes picking for bread.

From *Over the Garden Wall,* by Eleanor Farjeon. Copyright, 1933, by Eleanor Farjeon. Reprinted by permission of the publishers, J. B. Lippincott Company.

# KITTEN'S NIGHT THOUGHTS

### Oliver Herford

*Girls*
When Human Folk put out the light
*Boys*
And think they've made it dark as night,
*Solo 1*
A pussy cat sees every bit
*All*
As well as when the lights are lit.

*Boys*
When Human Folk have gone upstairs
*Girls*
And shed their skins and said their prayers,
*Solo 2*
And there is no one to annoy,
*All*
Then Pussy may her life enjoy.

*Row 1*
No human hands to pinch or slap,
*Row 2*
Or rub her fur against the nap,
*Row 3*
Or throw cold water from a pail,
*Row 4*
Or make a handle of her tail.

*Solo 3*
And so you will not think it wrong,
*Row 5*
When she can play the whole night long,
*Row 6*
With no one to disturb her play,
*All*
That Pussy goes to bed by day.

Reprinted from *Kitten's Garden of Verses*, by Oliver Herford. Copyright, 1911, by Oliver Herford; 1939, by Beatrice Herford Hayward. Used by permission of the publishers, Charles Scribner's Sons.

# THE KITTY

### Elizabeth Prentiss

*All*
Once there was a little kitty
*Girls*
Whiter than snow;
*Boys*
In a barn she used to frolic,
*All*
Long time ago.

*Boys*
In the barn a little mousie
Ran to and fro;
For she heard the kitty coming,
Long time ago.

*Girls*
Two eyes had little kitty,
Black as a sloe;
And they spied the little mousie,
Long time ago.

*All*
Four paws had little kitty,
*Girls*
Paws soft as dough,
*Boys*
And they caught the little mousie,
*All*
Long time ago.

*Solo 1*
Nine teeth had little kitty,
*All*
All in a row;
*Boys*
And they bit the little mousie,
*Girls*
Long time ago.

*Boys*
When the teeth bit little mousie,
*Girls*         *Solo 2*
Little mouse cried "Oh!"
*Boys*
But she got away from kitty,
*All*
Long time ago.

## MICE

### Rose Fyleman

*Solo 1*
I think mice
Are rather nice.

*Row 1*
Their tails are long,
*Row 2*
Their faces small,
*Row 3*
They haven't any
Chins at all.
*Row 4*
Their ears are pink
*Row 5*
Their teeth are white,
*Row 6*
They run about
The house at night.
*Girls*
They nibble things
They shouldn't touch,
*Boys*
And no one seems
To like them much.

*All*
But I think mice
Are nice.

From *Fifty-One New Nursery Rhymes*, by Rose Fyleman. Copyright, 1932, by Doubleday and Company, Inc.

# MARY MIDDLING

### Rose Fyleman

*Solo*
Mary Middling had a pig
*Row 1     Row 2*
Not very little and not very big,
*Row 3     Row 4*
Not very pink, not very green,
*Row 5     Row 6*
Not very dirty, not very clean,

*Row 1     Row 2*
Not very good, not very naughty,
*Row 3     Row 4*
Not very humble, not very haughty,
*Row 5     Row 6*
Not very thin, not very fat;
*All*
Now what would you give for a pig like that?

From *Fifty-One New Nursery Rhymes,* by Rose Fyleman. Copyright, 1932, by Doubleday and Company, Inc.


# MOUSE

### Hilda Conkling

*Girls*
Little mouse in gray velvet,
*All*
Have you had a cheese breakfast?
*Boys*
There are no crumbs on your coat,
*All*
Did you use a napkin?
*Boys*
I wonder what you had to eat,
*Girls*
And who dresses you in gray velvet.

From *Poems by a Little Girl,* by Hilda Conkling. Copyright, 1920, by J. B. Lippincott Company, and reprinted with their permission.

# THE MILKMAN'S HORSE

#### Author Unknown

*Girls*
On summer mornings when it's hot,
*Boys*
The milkman's horse can't even trot;
*All*
But pokes along like this——
*Solo 1*
Klip-klop, Klip-klop, Klip-klop.

*Girls*
But in the winter brisk,
*Boys*
He perks right up and wants to frisk;
*All*
And then he goes like this——
*Solo 2*
Klippity-klip, Klippity-klip, Klippity-klip.


# MORAL SONG

#### John Farrar

*Solo 1*
Oh, so cool
*Boys*
In his deep green pool
*Girls*            *All*
Was a frog on a log one day!
*Solo 2*
He would blink his eyes
As he snapped at flies,
*Girls*
For his mother was away,
*All*
For his mother was away!

*Solo 3*
Now that naughty frog
Left his own home log
*Boys*
And started out to play.
*Girls         Boys*
He flipped and he flopped
*All*
And he never stopped
*Boys*
Till he reached the great blue bay,
*All*
Till he reached the great blue bay!

*Girls*
Alas, with a swish
*Boys*
Came a mighty fish,
*All*
And swallowed him where he lay.
*Solo 4*
Now it's things like this
That never miss
*All*
Little frogs who don't obey,
*Solo 4*
Little frogs who don't obey!

From *Songs for Parents,* by John Farrar, published by Yale University Press.

## MY DOG

### Marchette Gaylord Chute

*Girls*
His nose is short and scrubby;
*Boys*
His ears hang rather low;
*Solo 1*
And he always brings the stick back,
*All*
No matter how far you throw.

*Girls*
He gets spanked rather often
*Boys*
For things he shouldn't do,
*Girls*          *Boys*
Like lying on beds, and barking,
*All*
And eating up shoes when they're new.

*Boys*
He always wants to be going
Where he isn't supposed to go.
*Girls*
He tracks up the house when it's snowing—
*Solo 2*
Oh, puppy, I love you so!

From *Rhymes About Ourselves*, by Marchette Gaylord Chute. Used by permission of the publishers, The Macmillan Company.

## ONCE I SAW A LITTLE BIRD

### Author Unknown

*Solo 1*
Once I saw a little bird
*All*
Come hop, hop, hop.
*Solo 1*     *Solo 2*
So I cried, "Little bird,
Will you stop, stop, stop?"

*Solo 1*
I was going to the window
*Solo 2*
To say, "How do you do?"
*Boys*
But he shook his little tail,
*All*
And away he flew.

# THE NAUGHTY LITTLE ROBIN

### Phoebe Cary

*Solo 1*
Once there was a robin,
*All*
Lived outside a door;
*Girls*
He wanted to go inside
*Boys*
And hop upon the floor.

*Solo 2*
"Oh, no," said mother robin,
"You must stay with me;
*All*
Little birds are safest
Sitting in a tree."

*Solo 3*
"I do not care," said the robin,
*All*
And he gave his tail a fling.
*Solo 3*
"I do not think the old folks
Know quite everything."

*Girls*        *Solo 4*
Down he flew, and kitty caught him
*All*
Quicker than a wink:
*Solo 5*
"Oh," he cried, "I'm very sorry,
But I did not think."

# THE PIGEONS

### Maud Burnham

*Girls*
Ten snowy white pigeons are standing in line,
*All*
On the roof of the barn in the warm sunshine.

*Boys*
Ten snowy white pigeons fly down to the ground,
*All*
To eat of the grain that is thrown all around.

*Girls*
Ten snowy white pigeons soon flutter aloof,
*All*
And sit in a line on the edge of the roof.

*Boy*                          *Girls*
Ten pigeons are saying politely, "Thank you!"
*Girl*                         *Boys*
If you listen, you hear their gentle, "Coo—roo!"

Reprinted by permission of the publishers, Milton Bradley Company.


# THE NEW BABY CALF

### Edith H. Newlin

*All*
Buttercup, the cow, had a new baby calf,
*Girls*
A fine baby calf,
*Boys*
A strong baby calf,
*Solo 1*
Not strong like his mother,
*Boys*
But strong for a calf,
*All*
For *this* baby calf was so *new!*

*Row 1*
Buttercup licked him with her strong warm tongue,
*Row 2*
Buttercup washed him with her strong warm tongue,
*Row 3*
Buttercup brushed him with her strong warm tongue,
*All*
And the new baby calf *liked that!*

*Row 4*
The new baby calf took a very little walk,
*Girls*
A tiny little walk,
*Solo 2*
A teeny little walk,
*Boys*
But his long legs wobbled
When he took a little walk,
*All*
And the new baby calf fell down.

*Solo 3*
Buttercup told him with a low soft "Moo-oo!"
*Boys*
That he was doing very well for one so very new
*Girls*
And she talked very gently, as other cows do,
*All*
And the new baby calf *liked* that!

*Row 5*
The new baby calf took another little walk,
*Girls*
A little longer walk,
*Boys*
A little stronger walk,
*Row 6*
He walked around his mother and he found the place to drink
*All*
And the new baby calf liked *that!*

*Solo 4*
The new baby calf drank milk every day,
*Girls*
His legs grew so strong that he could run and play,
*Boys*
He learned to eat grass and then grain and hay,
*All*
And the big baby calf grew fat!


# THE RABBIT

### Edith King

*All*
Brown bunny sits inside his burrow
*Solo 1*
Till everything is still,
*Girls*
Then out he slips along the furrow,
*All*
Or up the grassy hill.

*Girls*
He nibbles all about the bushes,
*Boys*
Or sits to wash his face,
*Solo 2*
But at a sound he stamps, and rushes
*All*
At a surprising pace.

*Girls*
You see some little streaks and flashes,
*Solo 3*
A last sharp twink of white,
*Boys*
And down his hidy-hole he dashes
*All*
And disappears from sight.

From *Fifty New Poems for Children*, reprinted by special permission of Basil Blackwell and Mott, Ltd., Oxford, England.

# ROBIN

### Tom Robinson

*Boys*
Hop and skip
On the lawn,
*Girls*
Robin Red Breast—
Come and gone.

*All*
You skip so fast
Along the ground,
*Boys*
Stop, hop and stop,
*Girls*
Look around.

*Solo 1*
Hi, spy!
*All*
At your feet
A big fat worm!
*Boys*
Sweet to eat!

*Row 1*
Bob your head,
*Row 2*
Catch him quick!
*Row 3*
Pull and haul,
*Row 4*
Tug and strain
With might and main,
*Row 5*
Gulp and swallow,
*Row 6*
That is all.
*All*
Very slick!

*Girls*
Skip and hop,
*Boys*
Run and stop,
*All*
Look around
On the ground.

*Solo 2*
Hi, spy!
*All*
With might and main
What you did
You do again.

From *In and Out*, by Tom Robinson. Copyright, 1943, by Tom Robinson. Reprinted by permission of The Viking Press, Inc., New York.

## PRECOCIOUS PIGGY

### Thomas Hood

*All*
"Where are you going, you little pig?"
*Solo 1*
"I'm leaving my mother, I'm growing so big!"
*Girls*
"So big, young pig,
*Boys*
So young, so big!
*All*
What, leaving your mother, you foolish young pig!"

*Girls*
"Where are you going, you little pig?"
*Solo 1*
"I've got a new spade, and I'm going to dig."
*All*
"To dig, little pig?
*Solo 2*
A little pig dig!
*All*
Well, I never saw a pig with a spade that could dig!"

*Boys*
"Where are you going, you little pig?"
*Solo 1*
"Why, I'm going to have a nice ride in a gig!"
*Girls*
"In a gig, little pig?
*Boys*
What, a pig in a gig!
*All*
Well, I never saw a pig ride in a gig!"

"Where are you going, you little pig?"
*Solo 1*
"Well, I'm going to the ball to dance a fine jig!"
*Girls*
"A jig, little pig!
*Boys*
A pig dance a jig!
*All*
Well, I never before saw a pig dance a jig!"

*Girls*
"Where are you going, you little pig?"
*Solo 1*
"I'm going to the fair to run a fine rig."
*All*
"A rig, little pig!
*Solo 3*
A pig run a rig!
*All*
Well, I never before saw a pig run a rig!"

*Boys*
"Where are you going, you little pig?"
*Solo 1*
"I'm going to the barber's to buy me a wig!"
*Girls*
"A wig, little pig!
*Boys*
A pig in a wig!
*All*
Why, whoever before saw a pig in a wig!"

# THE QUARRELSOME KITTENS

##### Anonymous

*Duet              All*
Two little kittens one stormy night,
*Girls             Boys*
Began to quarrel, and then to fight;
*Girls             Boys*
One had a mouse, the other had none,
*All*
And that's the way the quarrel begun.
*Boy              Boys*
"I'll have that mouse," said the biggest cat,

*Girl*
"You'll have that mouse?
*Girls*
We'll see about that!"
*Boy              Boys*
"I *will* have that mouse," said the eldest son;
*Girl              Girls*
"You shan't have that mouse," said the little one.

*Solo 1          Boys*
I told you before 'twas a stormy night
When these two little kittens began to fight;
*Girls*
The old woman seized her sweeping broom,
*All*
And swept the two kittens right out of the room.

*Girls*
The ground was covered with frost and snow,
*Duet*
And the two little kittens had nowhere to go.
*Boys*
So they laid them down on the mat at the door
*All*
When the old woman finished sweeping the floor.

*Duet*
Then they crept in, as quiet as mice,
*Boys*
All wet with snow and as cold as ice;
*Girls*
For they found it was better,
That stormy night,
*All*
To lie down and sleep
Than to quarrel and fight.

## THE SWALLOW

### Christina Rossetti

*Boys*
Fly away, fly away over the sea,
*Girls*
Sun loving swallow, for summer is done;
*Solo*
Come again, come again, come back to me,
*All*
Bringing the summer, and bringing the sun.

Reprinted by permission of the publishers, Little, Brown and Company.

## THE SQUIRREL

### Author Unknown

*Row 1   Row 2*
Whisky, frisky,
*Row 3*
Hippity hop,
*All*
Up he goes
To the tree top!
*Row 4   Row 5*
Whirly, twirly,
*Row 6*
Round and round,
*All*
Down he scampers
To the ground.

*Boys    Girls*
Furly, curly
*Boy*
What a tail!
*Girls*
Tall as a feather
*Boys*
Broad as a sail!
*Teacher*
Where's his supper?
*All*
In the shell,
*Girls    Boys*
Snappity, crackity,
*All*
Out it fell.


# THE ROBIN

### Laurence Alma-Tadema

*Solo 1*
When father takes his spade to dig
*All*
Then Robin comes along;
*Boys*
And sits upon a little twig
*Girls*
And sings a little song.

*Solo 2*
Or, if the trees are rather far,
*Girls*
He does not stay alone,
*Boys*
But comes up close to where we are
*All*
And bobs upon a stone.

# RABBITS

## Dorothy Baruch

*Solo 1*
My two white rabbits chase each other
*All*
With humping, bumping backs.
*Boys*
They go hopping, hopping,
*Solo 2*
And their long ears
*Girls*
Go flopping, flopping.
*All*
And they make faces with their noses
*Solo 3*
Up and down.

*Solo 4*
Today
I went inside their fence
To play rabbit with them.
*Boys*
And in one corner
*Girls*
Under a loose bush
*Solo 5*
I saw something shivering the leaves.
And I pushed and looked.
And I found——
*Boys*
There in a hole in the ground——
*Trio*
Three baby rabbits
*Girls*
HIDDEN away.
*Solo 6      All*
And THEY made faces with their noses
Up and down.

Reprinted by special permission of the author, and of Harper and Brothers, publishers.

# THE LITTLE TURTLE

### Vachel Lindsay

*All*
There was a little turtle.
*Row 1*
He lived in a box.
*Row 2*
He swam in a puddle.
*Row 3*
He climbed on the rocks.

*Row 4*
He snapped at a mosquito.
*Row 5*
He snapped at a flea.
*Row 6*
He snapped at a minnow.
*Solo*
And he snapped at me.

*Girls*
He caught the mosquito.
*Boys*
He caught the flea.
*All*
He caught the minnow.
*Solo*
But he didn't catch me.

From *Collected Poems* by Vachel Lindsay, by permission of The Macmillan Company, publishers.

# WILD BEASTS

### Evaleen Stein

*Solo 1*
I will be a lion
And you shall be a bear,
*Duet*
And each of us shall have a den
*All*
Beneath a nursery chair;

*Solo 2*
And you must growl, and growl, and growl,
*Solo 3*
And I will roar and roar,
*Girls    Boys    All*
And then—why, then—you'll growl again,
*Solo 4*
And I will roar some more.

From *Child Songs of Cheer*, by Evaleen Stein. Copyright, 1918, by Lothrop, Lee and Shepard Company, and used with their permission.

## TIME TO RISE

### R. L. STEVENSON

*All*
A birdie with a yellow bill
*Boys*
Hopped upon the window sill,
*Girls*
Cocked his shiny eye and said:
*Solo*
"Ain't you 'shamed, you sleepyhead?"

## WHAT DOES LITTLE BIRDIE SAY?

### ALFRED TENNYSON

*Girls*
What does little birdie say
In her nest at peep of day?
*Solo 1    Boys*
"Let me fly," says little birdie,
*All*
"Mother, let me fly away."

*Solo 2*
"Birdie, rest a little longer,
Till the little wings are stronger."
*All*
So she rests a little longer,
Then she flies away.

*Boys*
What does little baby say,
In her bed at peep of day?
*Girls*
Baby says, like little birdie,
*All*
"Let me rise and fly away."

*Solo 3*
"Baby, sleep a little longer,
Till the little limbs are stronger."
*All*
If she sleeps a little longer,
Baby, too, shall fly away.

## THREE LITTLE KITTENS

### Eliza Lee Follen

*All*
Three little kittens they lost their mittens;
And they began to cry,
*Trio*
"Oh, mother dear, we very much fear
Our mittens we have lost."

*Solo 1*
"What! lost your mittens, you naughty kittens!
*All*
Then you shall have no pie."
*Trio*
"Mee-ow, mee-ow, mee-ow, mee-ow."
*Solo 2*
"No, you shall have no pie."

*Boys*
The three little kittens they found their mittens;
*Girls*
And they began to cry,
*Trio*
"Oh, mother dear, see here, see here!
Our mittens we have found."

*Solo 3*
"What! found your mittens! you good little kittens,
Now you shall have some pie."
*Trio*
"Purr, purr, purr, purr,
*All*
Purr, purr, purr."


## THE WOODPECKER

### Elizabeth Madox Roberts

*Girls*
The woodpecker pecked out a little round hole
*All*
And made him a house in a telephone pole.
*Solo*  *Boys*
One day when I watched he poked out his head,
*All*
And he had on a hood and a collar of red.

*Boys*
When the streams of rain pour out of the sky,
*Girls*
And the sparkles of lightning go flashing by,
*Boys*
And the big, big wheels of thunder roll,
*All*
He can snuggle back in the telephone pole.

From *Under the Tree*, by Elizabeth Madox Roberts. Copyright, 1922, by B. W. Huebsch, Inc. Reprinted by permission of The Viking Press, Inc., New York.

# NATURE AND SEASONS

# COVER

### Frances M. Frost

*Row 1*
Red leaves flutter,
*Row 2*
Yellow leaves fall,
*Row 3*
Brown leaves gather
*All*
Along a wall.

*Row 4*
Brown leaves huddle
Against the gray
Stones some farmer
Set one way

Between two pastures.
*Row 5*
Curled leaves keep
Any wall warm
*All*
When winter's deep.

From *Hemlock Hall*, Vol. 27, in the *Yale Series of Younger Poets*. Reprinted with permission of the author and of Yale University Press.


# THE BIRCHES

### Walter Prichard Eaton

*Girls*
The little birches, white and slim,
*All*
Gleaming in the forest dim,
*Boys*
Must think the day is almost gone,
*Solo*
For each one has her nightie on.

From *Echoes and Realities*, by Walter Prichard Eaton. Copyright, 1918, by Doubleday and Company, Inc.

# CATKIN

### Author Unknown

*Solo 1*
I have a little pussy,
*Girls*
And her coat is silver gray;
*Boys*
She lives in a great wide meadow
*All*
And she never runs away.

*Girls*
She always is a pussy,
*Boys*
She'll never be a cat
*Solo 2*
Because—she's a pussy willow!
*All*
Now what do you think of that?


# A DEWDROP

### Frank Dempster Sherman

*Girls*
Little drop of dew,
Like a gem you are;
*Boy*
I believe that you
*All*
Must have been a star.

*Boys*
When the day is bright,
On the grass you lie;
*Girl*
Tell me then, at night
*All*
Are you in the sky?

Reprinted by special arrangement with the author, and with the publishers, Houghton Mifflin Company.

# CRESCENT MOON

### Elizabeth Madox Roberts

*All            Boy*
And Dick said, "Look what I have found!"
*Girls*
And when we saw we danced around,
*Boys*
And made our feet just tip the ground.

*Girls*
We skipped our toes and sang, "Oh-lo.
*Boys*
Oh-who, oh-who, oh what do you know!
*All*
Oh-who, oh-hi, oh-loo, kee-low!"

*Girls*
We clapped our hands and sang, "Oh-ee!"
*All*
It made us jump and laugh to see
The little new moon above the tree.

From *Under the Tree,* by Elizabeth Madox Roberts. Copyright, 1922, by B. W. Huebsch. Used by permission of The Viking Press, Inc., New York.

# THE DANDELION

### Mrs. E. J. H. Goodfellow

*Girls*
There was a pretty dandelion,
With lovely, fluffy hair,
*All*
That glistened in the sunshine
And in the summer air.

*Boys*
But, oh! this pretty dandelion
Soon grew quite old and gray,
*All*
And, sad to tell, her charming hair
Blew many miles away.

## FROZEN MILK BOTTLES

### Olive Beaupré Miller

*Girls*
When old thermometer says zero,
*Solo*
Or something (Br-r-r) like that,
*Boys*
The milk-man's bottles at our door
*All*
Wear each a stovepipe hat.

Reprinted by permission of the author.


## THE DANDELION

### Author Unknown

*Girls*
O dandelion, yellow as gold,
What do you do all day?
*Solo 1*
I just wait here in the tall green grass
*All*
Till the children come to play.

*Boys*
O dandelion, yellow as gold,
What do you do all night?
*Solo 2*
I wait and wait till the cool dews fall
And my hair grows long and white.

*Girls*
And what do you do when your hair is white,
*Boys*
And the children come to play?
*Solo 3*
They take me up in their dimpled hands,
*All*
And blow my hair away.

## THE LITTLE PLANT

### Kate Louise Brown

*Girls*
In the heart of a seed,
*Boys*
Buried deep, so deep!
*All*
A dear little plant
Lay fast asleep!

*Solo 1    Girls*
"Wake!" said the sunshine,
*Solo 1*
"And creep to the light!"
*Solo 2    Boys*
"Wake!" said the voice
Of the raindrops bright.

*Girls*
The little plant heard
*Boys*
And it rose to see
*All*
What the wonderful
Outside world might be!

By permission of Helen K. Bradbury, Princeton, New Jersey.

## FIRST SNOW

### Marie Louise Allen

*Girls*
Snow makes whiteness where it falls.
*Boys*
The bushes look like popcorn-balls.
*Solo*
The places where I always play
*All*
Look like somewhere else today.

From *A Pocketful of Rhymes*, by Marie Louise Allen. Copyright, 1939, by Harper and Brothers.

# RAIN

### Robert Louis Stevenson

*All*
The rain is raining all around,
*Girls*
It falls on field and tree,
*Boys*
It rains on the umbrellas here,
*All*
And on the ships at sea.

From *A Child's Garden of Verses,* by Robert Louis Stevenson. Reprinted by permission of The Macmillan Company, publishers.


# THE ICICLE

### Mrs. Henry Gordon Gale

*All*
An icicle hung on a red brick wall,
*Girls*          Solo 1
And it said to the sun, "I don't like you at all!"
    Solo 2   Solo 3   Solo 4
——Drip, drip, drip.
*Boys*          Solo 5
But the sun said, "Dear, you've a saucy tongue,
And you should remember, I'm old and you're young."
    *All*
——Drip, drip, drip.

*Boys*
But the icicle only cried the more,
*Girls*
Though the good sun smiled on it just as before,
*All*
Until at the end of the winter day,
*Solo 6*
It had cried its poor little self away!
    *Boys   Girls   Solo 7*
——Drip, drip, drip.

Reprinted by permission of Public School Publishing Company.

## MILK IN WINTER

### Rhoda W. Bacmeister

*Solo 1*
In the early, shivery dark
Of wintertime I wake
*All*
And hear the klinkey-klank
That our milk bottles make.

*Boys*
The empty bottles clatter,
*Girls*
Boots on the snow peep-peep,
*All*
The milkman's truck goes rumbling off,
*Solo 2*
And I go back to sleep.

*Solo 3*
When I get up for breakfast
*Boys*
The morning dark is gone,
*Girls*
But there's the milk outside the door
*All*
With tall ice-cream hats on!

From *Stories to Begin On,* by Rhoda W. Bacmeister. Published and copyright by E. P. Dutton & Company, Inc., New York. 1929, Dutton; 1940, Dutton, respectively.


## I WONDER

### Mrs. Schuyler Van Renssalaer

*Boys*
I wonder if the stars are fire,
*Girls*
Or if the stars are gold,
*Solo*
And if a little one should drop,
*All*
'T would burn my hand to hold?

# THE MOON

### Eliza Lee Follen

*All*
O look at the moon!
*Girls*
She is shining up there;
*Solo 1     All*
O mother, she looks
Like a lamp in the air.
*Girls*
Last week she was smaller,
*Boys*
And shaped like a bow;
*Solo 2*
But now she's grown bigger,
*All*
And round as an O.
*Girls     Boys*
Pretty moon, pretty moon.
*All*
How you shine on the door,
*Girls*
And make it all bright
*Solo 3*
On my nursery floor!
*All*
You shine on my playthings
And show me their place,
*Solo 4*
And I love to look up
At your pretty bright face.
*Girls*
And there is a star
Close by you, and maybe
*Boys*
That small twinkling star
*All*
Is your little baby.

# RAIN

### Helen Wing

*All*
I like to look out of my window and see
The rain dripping down on the leaves of a tree.
*Girls            Boys*
They shiver a little and bend in their places,
*All*
While old Mother Nature is washing their faces.

Reprinted by special arrangement with the author.


# THE MITTEN SONG

### Marie Louise Allen

*Boys*
"Thumbs in the thumb-place,
*Girls*
Fingers all together!"
*Solo 1*
This is the song
*All*
We sing in mitten-weather.
*Solo 2*
When it is cold,
*All*
It doesn't matter whether
*Boys*
Mittens are wool,
*Girls*
Or made of finest leather,
*Solo 3*
This is the song
*Girls*
We sing in mitten-weather:
*Boys*
"Thumbs in the thumb-place,
*All*
Fingers all together!"

From *A Pocketful of Rhymes,* by Marie Louise Allen. Copyright, 1939, by Harper and Brothers.

# THE MOON

### May Morgan

*Solo 1*
I like to sit on our doorsill,
*All*
And watch the place above the hill
Get lighter every minute till
The moon comes up all bright and still.

*Solo 2*
Sometimes he is so slow, I think
    *Girls*
He'll never come: then, in a wink,
*Boys*
Almost behind the big oak tree,
*All*
He pops right up, and smiles at me.

From *St. Nicholas Book of Verse*. Copyright, 1923, by the Century Company. Reprinted by permission of Appleton-Century-Crofts, Inc.


# MERRY SUNSHINE

### Anonymous

*All*
"Good-morning, Merry Sunshine,
*Solo 1*
How did you wake so soon,
*Girls*
You've scared the little stars away
*Boys*
And shined away the moon.
*Solo 2*
I saw you go to sleep last night
*All*
Before I ceased my playing;
*Girls*
How did you get 'way over there?
*Boys*
And where have you been staying?"

*Solo 3*
"I never go to sleep, dear child,
I just go round to see
*All*
My little children of the east,
Who rise and watch for me.
*Solo 4*
I waken all the birds and bees
And flowers on my way,
*Solo 5*
And now come back to see the child
*All*
Who stayed out late at play."

## RAINING

### Rhoda W. Bacmeister

*Solo 1     Duet     Trio*
It's raining, raining, raining,
*All*
And all the world is wet.
*Boys               Girls*
It rained last night, and now today
       *All*
It's raining, raining, yet!

*Solo 2   Solo 3   Solo 4   Solo 5*
Drip, drip, drip, drip,
*Quartet*
Leaking from the eaves,
*Row 1     Row 2     Row 3*
Pattering, splashing, and tapping
*All*
On the roof and the tulip tree's leaves.

*Girls*
The quick little raindrops in puddles
Are dancing up and down;
*Boys*
Rivers rush down the gutters,
Foamy and dirty and brown.

*Girls*
Drip, drip, patter and splash,
*All*
How fast the raindrops race—
*Boys*
Running down the windowpane
*All*
Cold against my face!

From *Stories to Begin On,* by Rhoda W. Bacmeister. Published and copyright by E. P. Dutton & Company, Inc., New York. 1929, Dutton; 1940, Dutton, respectively.

## THE TRAGEDY

### Anne Cooper

*Solo 1*
As I went out a-walking,
*All*
All on a summer's day,
*Solo 1*
I met a dandelion
*All*
Standing proudly in the way.

*Girls*
But something very dreadful
*Boys*
Must have happened over night;
*Solo 2*
When I passed that way next morning,
*All*
His hair had all turned white!

From *St. Nicholas Magazine.* Copyright, 1924, by The Century Company. Reprinted by permission of Appleton-Century-Crofts, Inc.

# SNOWFLAKES

### Mary Mapes Dodge

*Solo 1*
Little white feathers
Filling the air——
*Boys*
Little white feathers!
How came you there?

*Girls*
We came from the cloud-birds,
Flying so high,
Shaking their white wings
Up in the sky.

*Solo 2*
Little white feathers,
Swiftly you go!
*Boys*
Little white snowflakes,
I love you so!

*Girls*
We are swift because
We have work to do;
But look up at us,
And we will kiss you!

From *St. Nicholas Magazine,* by permission of Mary Mapes Dodge, and D. Appleton-Century Company, Inc., publishers.

# SNOWFLAKES

### Elizabeth L. Cleveland

*Girls*
Snowflakes falling through the air,
*All*
Falling, falling everywhere.

*Boys*
Twisting, turning, floating down,
*All*
Covering white the noisy town.

*Row 1*
Roofs are laden, window edges,
*Row 2*
Snow is sticking to the ledges.

*Solo 1*
All the streets are silent now.
*Boys*
Comes the shirring of the plow.

*Girls*
Clean behind it shines the track,
*All*
Cars are coming, click-a-clack.

*Row 3*
People shoveling, piling snow,
Making clear the way to go.

*Row 4*
Wagons crunch and autos whir,
Wheels that turn and never stir.

*Row 5*
Children run and slide and tumble,
*All*
Snow all over, not a grumble.

*Row 6*
Snowballs flying, dodge and run!
*All*
Here's a day of snowy fun!

## RAINDROPS

### Isla Paschal Richardson

*All*
I love to lie awake and hear
The pitter-patter of the rain;
*Solo 1*
I make believe it plays with me,
*Boys*
Tap-tapping on the windowpane!

*Solo 2*
In daytime, too, I love to see
The raindrops bounce upon the street;
*Girls*
They dance and skip like fairies gay,
*All*
With crystal slippers on their feet.

Reprinted by permission of *The Instructor*.

## ICE

### Dorothy Aldis

*All*
When it is the winter time
*Solo 1*
I run up the street
*Girls*
And I make the ice laugh
With my little feet——
*Boys*
"Crickle, crackle, crickle,
*Solo 2*
Crrreeet, crrreeet, crrreeet."

From *Everything and Anything*, by Dorothy Aldis. Copyright, 1925, 1926, 1927, by Dorothy Aldis. Courtesy of G. P. Putnam's Sons, New York.

# THE SNOWMAN

### Frances Frost

*All*
We made a snowman in our yard,
*Solo 1  Solo 2     Solo 3*
Jolly, and round, and fat.
*Boys*
We gave him father's pipe to smoke
*Girls*
And father's battered hat.
*Boys*
We tied a red scarf around his neck,
*Girls*
And in his buttonhole
We stuck a holly spray.
*Row 1*
He had black buttons made of coal
*Row 2          Row 3*
He had black eyes, a turned up nose,
*Row 4*
A wide and cheerful grin;
*Solo 4*
And there he stood in our front yard,
*All*
Inviting company in!


# SNOW

### Alice Wilkins

*All*
The snow fell softly all the night.
*Girls*
It made a blanket soft and white.
*Boys*
It covered houses, flowers, and ground,
*Solo*
But did not make a single sound.

From *The Golden Flute* (The John Day Company), by Alice Hubbard and Adeline Babbitt. By permission of Miss Hubbard.

## WISE JOHNNY

### Edwina Fallis

*Solo*
Little Johnny-jump-up said,
*All*
"It must be spring,
*Solo*
I just saw a lady-bug
*All*
And heard a robin sing."

Reprinted by arrangement with the author.

## SNOWSTORM

### Rhoda W. Bacmeister

*Solo 1*
Oh did you see the snow come?
So softly floating down,—
*Girls      Boys*
White in the air, white on the trees,
*All*
And white all over the ground!

*Boys*
It rattled gently on dry leaves;
*Solo 2*
It tickled on my face;
*Girls*
And spread its thick, soft cover
On every kind of place.

*All*
The autos standing in the street
Had snowy tops and lights,
*Solo 3*
And even on my mummy's hat
*All*
Was a big thick pile of white!

From *Stories to Begin On*, by Rhoda W. Bacmeister. Published and copyright by E. P. Dutton and Company, Inc., New York. 1929, Dutton; 1940, Dutton, respectively.

# RAIN IN THE NIGHT

### Amelia Josephine Burr

*Girls*
Raining, raining,
*All*
All night long,
*Boys        Girls*
Sometimes loud, sometimes soft,
*All*
Just like a song.

*Row 1*
There'll be rivers in the gutters
*Row 2*
And lakes along the street.
*All*
It will make our lazy kitty
Wash his dirty little feet.

*Row 3*
The roses will wear diamonds
*Row 4*
Like kings and queens at court;
*All*
But the pansies all get muddy
Because they are so short.

*Solo 1*
I'll sail my boat tomorrow
*All*
In wonderful new places,
*Solo 1*
But first I'll take my watering-pot
*All*
And wash the pansies' faces.

From *Selected Lyrics*, by Amelia Josephine Burr. Copyright, 1927, by Doubleday and Company, Inc.

## WHEN BLUE SKY SMILES

### Olive Beaupré Miller

*Boys*
When blue sky smiles and birds come back,
*Girls*
And little flowers are springing,
*Solo*
I feel inside all shiny warm,
*All*
Like dancing and like singing.

Reprinted by permission of the author.

## MOON, SO ROUND AND YELLOW

### Matthias Barr

*All*
Moon, so round and yellow,
Looking from on high,
*Girls*
How I love to see you
Shining in the sky.
*Boys*
Oft and oft I wonder,
When I see you there,
*All*
How they get to light you,
Hanging in the air;

*Boys*
Where you go at morning,
When the night is past,
*Girls*
And the sun comes peeping
O'er the hills at last.
*Solo*
Sometime I will watch you
Slyly overhead,
*All*
When you think I'm sleeping
Snugly in my bed.

# JACK FROST
### Author Unknown

*Solo 1*                *All*
When Jack Frost comes—oh! the fun!
*Boys*
He plays his pranks on everyone.
*Girls*
He'll pinch your nose and bite your toes,
*All*
But where he goes—nobody knows.

*Boys*
He paints upon the window-pane,
Tin soldiers, teddy-bears, and trains,
*Girls*
He nips the leaves from off the trees——
*All*
This little man—nobody sees.


# THE RUNAWAY BROOK
### Eliza Lee Follen

*Solo 1*
"Stop, stop, pretty water!"
*All*
Said Mary one day,
*Girls*
To a frolicsome brook
*Boys*
That was running away.

*All*
"You run on so fast!
*Solo 1*
I wish you would stay!
*Girls*
My boat and flowers
*All*
You will carry away.

*Solo 1*
"But I will run after;
Mother says that I may;
*All*
For I would know where
You are running away."

*Solo 2*
So Mary ran on;
But I have heard say
*All*
That she never could find
Where the brook ran away.


## PUSSY WILLOW

### Kate L. Brown

*Boys*
Pussy Willow wakened
From her Winter nap,
*Girls*
For the frolic Spring Breeze
On her door did tap.

*Solo 1*
Mistress Pussy Willow
Opened wide the door;
*All*
Never had the sunshine
Seemed so bright before.

*Solo 2*
Happy little children
Cried with laugh and shout,
*All*
"Spring is coming, coming,
Pussy Willow's out."

By permission of Helen K. Bradbury, Princeton, New Jersey.

# DANDELIONS

### Marietta W. Brewster

*Solo 1*
When I went out to play today
*All*
I found dandelions yellow and gay,
*Solo 2*
And then when I came in tonight
*All*
The dandelions had turned to white.

*Girls*
They were so round and so soft, too,
*Solo 3*
I picked one up and blew and blew,
*All*
And when I blew, why, do you know
The fluff came off—you try and blow!


# TWINKLE, TWINKLE, LITTLE STAR

### Jane and Anne Taylor

*All*
Twinkle, twinkle, little star,
*Solo 1*
How I wonder what you are!
*Girls*
Up above the world so high,
*All*
Like a diamond in the sky.

*Row 1*
When the blazing sun is set,
*Row 2*
And the grass with dew is wet,
*Rows 1 and 2*
Then you show your little light
Twinkle, twinkle, all the night.

*Row 3*
Then the traveler in the dark
*Row 4*
Thanks you for your tiny spark.
*Rows 3 and 4*
How could he see where to go
If you did not twinkle so?

*Boys*
In the dark-blue sky you keep,
*Solo 1*
And often through my curtains peep,
*Row 5*
For you never shut an eye,
Till the sun is in the sky.

*Row 6*
As your bright and tiny spark
Lights the traveler in the dark,
*Solo 1*
Though I know not what you are,
*All*
Twinkle, twinkle, little star.


## CLOUDS

### Author Unknown

*All*
White sheep, white sheep,
On a blue hill,
*Girls*
When the wind stops,
You all stand still.

*Boys*
When the wind blows,
You walk away slow.
*All*
White sheep, white sheep,
Where do you go?

## UNDER THE GROUND

### Rhoda W. Bacmeister

*Solo 1*
What is under the grass,
*Row 1*
Way down in the ground,
*Row 2*
Where everything is cool and wet
*All*
With darkness all around?

*Row 3*
Little pink worms live there;
*Row 4*
Ants and brown bugs creep
Softly round the stones and rocks
Where roots are pushing deep.

*Solo 2*
Do they hear us walking
*Row 5*
On the grass above their heads;
*Row 6*
Hear us running over
*All*
While they snuggle in their beds?

From *Stories to Begin On*, by Rhoda W. Bacmeister. Published and copyright by E. P. Dutton and Company, Inc., New York. 1929, Dutton; 1940, Dutton, respectively.

## THE PLAYING LEAVES

### Ora Clayton Moore

*Girls*
The leaves are all such happy things
*Boys*
Away up in the tree,
*Row 1     Row 2     Row 3*
They dance and play and wave their hands,
*Row 4*
And nod to you and me.

*Boys*
When Jack Frost comes and sets them free,
*Row 5*
They jump down to the ground
*Row 6*
And play all sorts of silly games,
*All*
And scamper all around.

*Girls*
Then Daddy rakes them in a pile,
*Boys*
And makes them blaze so high;
*Solo 1         All*
But Mother says they've turned to smoke,
To play up in the sky.

Reprinted by special arrangement with J. H. Shultz Company, publishers.


## MAY MORNING

### Marjorie Barrows

*All*
The cherry tree's shedding
Its blossoms of May;
*Girls*
Does a fairyland wedding
Take place today?

*Boys*
Baby birds are coming
And learning to sing,
*All*
And the garden's all humming
With spring.

Reprinted by arrangement with the author.

# THE WHITE WINDOW

### JAMES STEPHENS

*All*
The Moon comes every night to peep
*Solo 1*
Through the window where I lie;
*All*
But I pretend to be asleep;
*Boys*
And watch the Moon go slowly by,
*Girls*
And she never makes a sound!

*Girl*        *All*
She stands and stares! And then she goes
*Solo 2*
To the house that's next to me,
*Row 1*
Stealing by on tippy-toes;
*Row 2*
To peek at folk asleep maybe
*Boys*
And she never makes a sound!

From *Collected Poems*, by James Stephens. By permission of The Macmillan Company, publishers.

# WHERE DO ALL THE DAISIES GO?

### ANONYMOUS

*Teacher*
Where do all the daisies go?
*Girl 1   Boy 1*
I know, I know!
*Row 1*
Underneath the snow they creep,
*Row 2*
Nod their little heads and sleep,
*Girls*
In the springtime out they peep;
*All*
That is where they go!

*Teacher*
Where do all the birdies go?
*Boy 2   Girl 2*
I know, I know!
*Row 3*
Far away from winter snow,
To the fair, warm South they go,
*Boys*
Where they stay till daisies blow;
*All*
That is where they go!

*Teacher*
Where do all the babies go?
*Girls   Boys*
I know, I know!
*Girls*
In the glancing firelight warm,
*Boys*
Safely sheltered from all harm,
*Girl 3*
Soft they lie on mother's arm;
*All*
That is where they go!

# PEOPLE

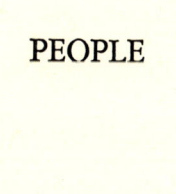

# TO BABY

### Kate Greenaway

*Solo 1*
Oh, what shall my blue eyes go see,
*Row 1*
Shall it be pretty quack-quack today?
*Row 2*
Or the peacock upon the yew tree?
*Row 3*
Or the dear little white lambs at play?
*All*
Say, baby.

*Row 4*
For baby is such a young petsy,
*Row 5*
For baby is such a sweet dear.
*Row 6*
And baby is growing quite old now—
*All*
She's just getting on for a year.

Reprinted by permission of Frederick Warne and Company, Inc., publishers, New York.


# SLEEP, BABY, SLEEP

### Old Lullaby from the German

*Solo 1*
Sleep, baby, sleep!
*Boys*
Thy father watches the sheep.
*Girls*
Thy mother is shaking the dreamland tree,
*Solo 2*
And down falls a little dream for thee.
*All*
Sleep, baby, sleep!

*Solo 3*
Sleep, baby, sleep!
*Boys*
The large stars are the sheep;
*Solo 4*
The little stars are the lambs, I guess;
*Girls*
The bright moon is the shepherdess.
*All*
Sleep, baby, sleep!


## PATRICK GOES TO SCHOOL

### Alicia Aspinwall

*Solo 1*
"I'm going to school tomorrow, just
*Girls*
To learn to write and read.
*Solo 1*
I wish I didn't have to, for
*Boys*
I do not see the need."


*Solo 2*     *All*     *Solo 2*
"Do you want to be," said Dad, "a deep-
Dyed ig-no-ra-mus, Pat?"
*Solo 1*
"Oh, no!" I cried. "I'd hate to be
*Boys*
A dreadful thing like *that!*"


*Solo 1*
"And so I thought I'd go to school
*Girls*
To learn to read and write.
*Boys*
So *not* to be that 'deep-dyed' thing
Dad spoke about tonight."

From *Short Poems for Short People*, by Alicia Aspinwall. Published and copyright by E. P. Dutton and Company, Inc., New York. 1929, Dutton; 1940, Dutton, respectively.

# MOTHER

### Rose Fyleman

*All*
When mother comes each morning
*Row 1*
She wears her oldest things,
*Row 2*
She doesn't make a rustle,
*Row 3*
She hasn't any rings;
*Solo 1    Solo 2*
She says, "Good morning, chickies,
It's such a lovely day,
Let's go into the garden
*All*
And have a game of play."

*Girls*
When mother comes at teatime
*Row 4*
Her dress goes shoo-shoo-shoo,
*Row 5*
She always has a little bag,
*Row 6*
Sometimes a sunshade, too;
*Solo 3    Solo 4*
She says, "I am so hoping
There's something left for me;
*All*
Please hurry up, dear Nanna,
*Solo 4*
I'm dying for my tea."

*Boys*
When mother comes at bedtime
*Girls*
Her evening dress she wears,
*Solo 5*
She tells us each a story
*All*
When we have said our prayers;

*Girls*
And if there is a party
*Boys*
She looks so shiny bright
*All*
It's like a lovely fairy
Dropped in to say good night.

From *Fairies and Chimneys*, by Rose Fyleman. Copyright, 1920, by Doubleday and Company, Inc.

## MRS. BROWN

### Rose Fyleman

*Girl 1*
As soon as I'm in bed at night
*All*
And snugly settled down,
*Girl 1*
The little girl I am by day
*All*
Goes very suddenly away,
*Girl 1*
And then I'm Mrs. Brown.

*Girl 1*
I have a family of six,
*All*
And all of them have names,
*Boys        Girl 2   Girl 3*
The girls are Joyce and Nancy Maud,
*Girls         Boy 1      Boy 2*
The boys are Marmaduke and Claude
*Boy 3     Boy 4*
And Percival and James.

*All*
We have a house with twenty rooms
A mile away from town;
I think it's good for girls and boys
To be allowed to make a noise—
*Girl 4*
And so does Mrs. Brown.

*Boys*
We do the most exciting things,
*Girls*
Enough to make you creep;
*All*
And on and on and on we go—
*Girl 1*
I sometimes wonder if I know
When I have gone to sleep.

From *Fairy Green,* by Rose Fyleman. Copyright, 1923, by Doubleday and Company, Inc.

## MY POLICEMAN

### Rose Fyleman

*Row 1*
He is always standing there
*All*
At the corner of the square;
*Row 2*
He is very big and fine
*Row 3*
And his silver buttons shine.

*Row 4*
All the carts and taxis do
Everything he tells them to,
*Row 5*
And the little errand boys
When they pass him make no noise.

*Solo 1*
Though I seem so very small
I am not afraid at all;
*Duet*
He and I are friends, you see,
*All*
And he always smiles at me.

*Solo 2*
Once I wasn't very good
Rather near to where he stood,
*All*
But he never said a word
*Solo 3*
Though I'm sure he must have heard.

*Girls*
Nurse has a policeman, too,
*Solo 4*  *Solo 5*
(Hers has brown eyes, mine has blue,)
*Boys*
Hers is sometimes on a horse,
*Solo 6*  *All*
But I like mine best, of course.

From *Fairy Green,* by Rose Fyleman. Copyright, 1923, by Doubleday and Company, Inc.

# RELIGIOUS POETRY

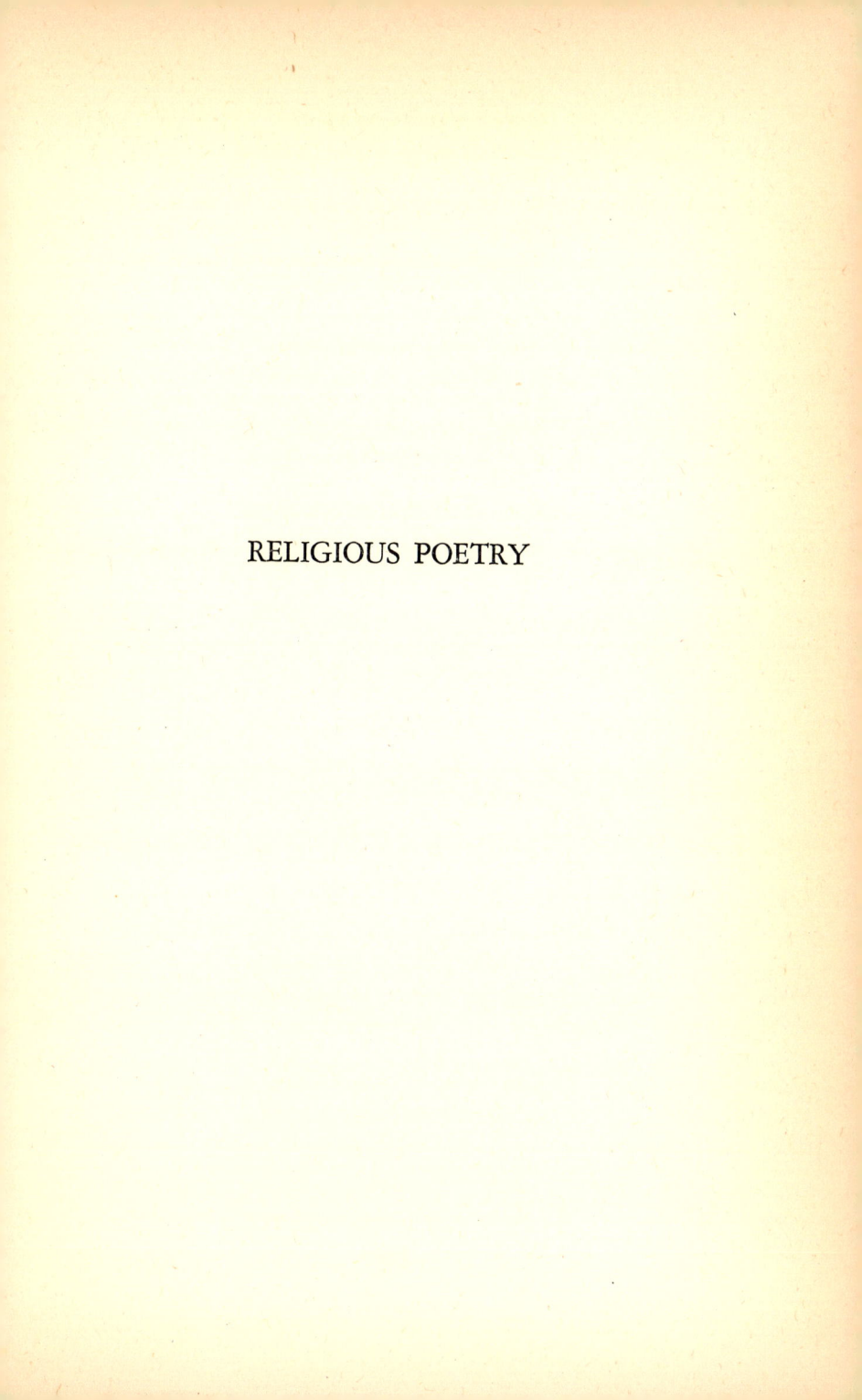

## BLESSING OVER FOOD

### H. N. Bialik. Translated by Jessie Sampter

*All*
Blest be God
*Solo*
Who did create
*Girls*
Porridge with milk,
*Boys*
A whole full plate;
*Girls*
And after porridge
Also an orange.

*All*
Oh, thanks to Him
*Boys*
From whom they came
*All*
Blessed be He
And blest His name.

From *Far Over the Sea,* reprinted by permission of the Union of American Hebrew Congregations, publishers.

## A CHILD'S GRACE

### Author Unknown

*Solo*
Thank you for the world so sweet,
*Boys*
Thank you for the food we eat,
*Girls*
Thank you for the birds that sing,
*All*
Thank you, God, for everything.

# EVENING HYMN

### Anonymous

*Solo 1*    *Solo 2*
I hear no voice, I feel no touch,
*Solo 3*
I see no glory bright;
*All*
But yet I know that God is near,
In darkness as in light.

*Solo 4*
He watches ever by my side,
*Solo 5*
And hears my whispered prayer;
*All*
The Father for His little child
Both night and day doth care.

# SPECIAL DAYS

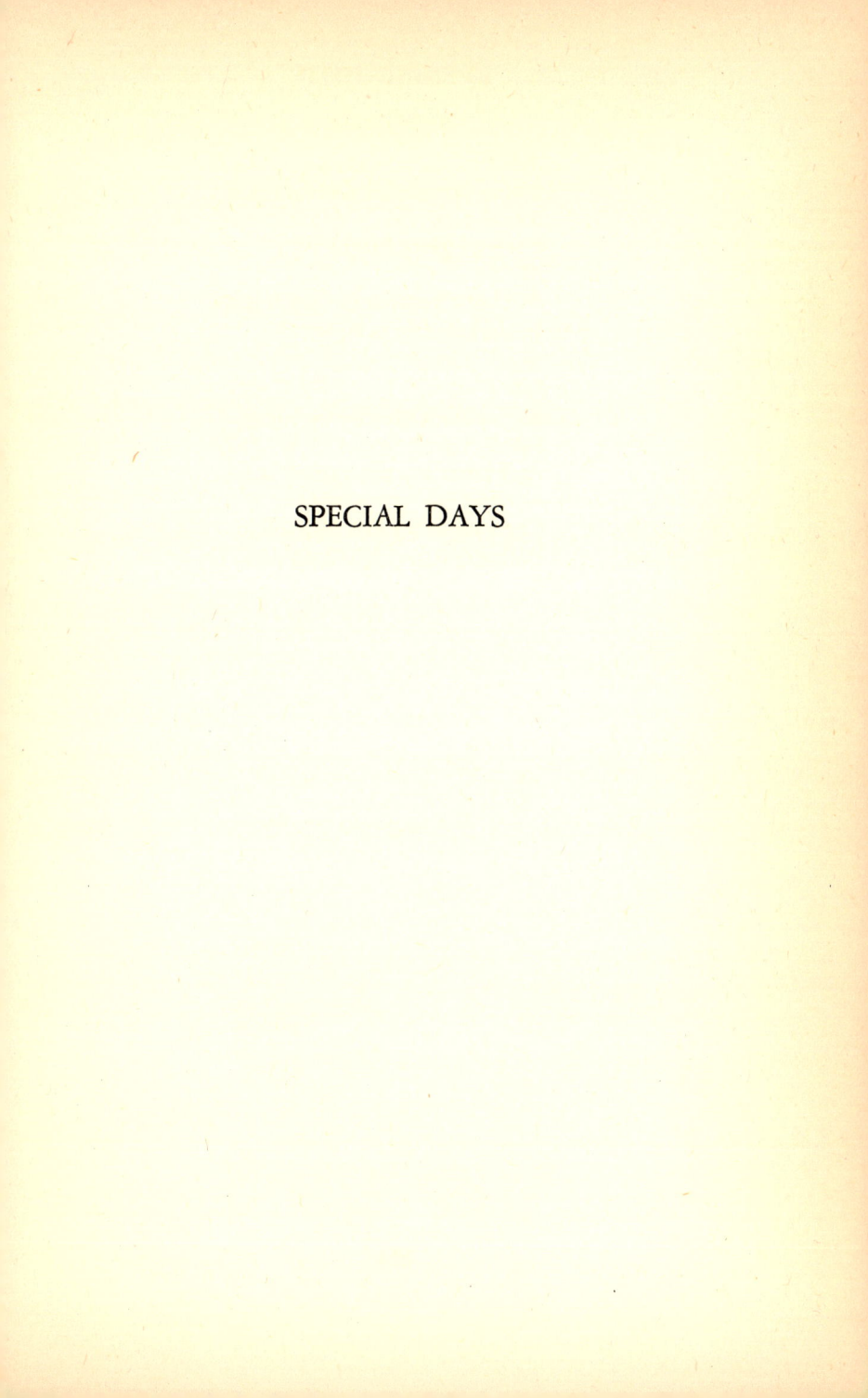

# A HALLOWEEN MEETING
### George O. Butler

*Solo 1*
I always thought, old witch,
*All*
That you were as bad as bad could be,
*Solo 1*
That if I ever met you
*All*
You would surely frighten me;
*Solo 1*　　　*Boys*
I don't believe that you can be
So very wicked, though,
*Girls*
Or else your owl and pussy cat
*All*
Could never love you so.

From *Merry Meet Again,* edited by Elizabeth Hough Sechrist, and reprinted by permission of the publishers, Macrae Smith Company.


# WAS SHE A WITCH
### Laura Elizabeth Richards

*Solo 1*
There was an old woman
*All*
Lived down in a dell;
*Solo 2*
She used to draw picklejacks
*All*
Out of the well.
*Solo 3*
How did she do it?
*All*
Nobody knew it,
*Girls*　　　*Boys*　　　*All*
She never, no never, no never would tell.

From *Tirra Lirra,* by Laura E. Richards. Copyright, 1918, 1930, 1932, by Laura E. Richards. Reprinted by permission of Little, Brown and Company.

# WHY DO THE BELLS OF CHRISTMAS RING?

### Eugene Field

*Girls*
Why do the bells of Christmas ring?
*All*
Why do little children sing?

*Solo 1*
Once a lovely shining star,
*Boys*
Seen by shepherds from afar,
*Solo 2*
Gently moved until its light
*All*
Made a manger's cradle bright.

*Solo 3*
There a darling baby lay
Pillowed soft upon the hay;
*Solo 4*
And its mother sang and smiled;
"This is Christ, the holy Child!"

*Boys*
Therefore bells for Christmas ring,
*All*
Therefore little children sing.

Reprinted from *Sharps and Flats,* by Eugene Field. Copyright, 1900, 1901, by Julia Sutherland Field; 1928, by Julia Sutherland Field; used by permission of the publishers, Charles Scribner's Sons.

# MY VALENTINE

### Mary Catherine Parsons

*Solo 1*
I have a little valentine
That someone sent to me.
*Girls*
It's pink and white and red and blue,
*All*
And pretty as can be.

*Row 1*
Forget-me-nots are round the edge,
*Row 2*
And tiny roses, too;
*Row 3*
And such a lovely piece of lace—
The very palest blue.

*Row 4*
And in the center there's a heart
As red as red can be!
*All*
And on it's written all in gold,
*Solo 2*
"To you, with Love from Me."


## THE SECRET

### Helen Cowles Le Cron

*Solo 1*                  *All*
"Where did they come from?" said Peter to Jane.
*Girls*
"Easter Eggs yellow and white,
*Boys*                 *All*
Scarlet and purple and spotted? It's plain
Somebody left them last night!"

*Solo 2*
The brown Easter Bunny that sat on the shelf
*All*
Was silent as silent could be,
*Solo 3*
But did I just dream that he smiled to himself?
           *All*
I thought so, but couldn't quite see.

Reprinted by permission of the author.

# RIDDLE: WHAT AM I?

### Dorothy Aldis

*Solo 1*
They chose me from my brothers:
*All*
"That's the nicest one," they said,
*Solo 1*
And they carved me out a face and put a
Candle in my head;

*Solo 2*
And they set me on the doorstep.
*Boys*
Oh, the night was dark and wild;
*Girls*  *Solo 2*
But when they lit the candle, then I
Smiled!

From *Hop, Skip and Jump*, by Dorothy Aldis. Copyright, 1934, by Dorothy Aldis. Courtesy of G. P. Putnam's Sons, New York.

# WHEN SANTA CLAUS COMES

### Author Unknown

*All*  *Solo 1*
A good time is coming, I wish it were here,
*All*
The very best time in the whole of the year;
*Solo 2*
I'm counting the time on my fingers and thumbs—
*All*
The weeks that must pass before Santa Claus comes.

*Girls*
Then when the first snowflakes begin to come down,
*Boys*
And the wind whistles sharp and the branches are brown,
*Solo 3*
I'll not mind the cold, though my fingers it numbs,
*All*
For it brings the time nearer when Santa Claus comes.

# BUNDLES

### John Farrar

*Girls*
A bundle is a funny thing,
*All*
It always sets me wondering;
*Boys*
For whether it is thin or wide
*All*
You never know just what's inside.

*Solo*
Especially on Christmas week,
*Girls*
Temptation is so great to peek!
*Boys*
Now wouldn't it be much more fun
*All*
If shoppers carried things undone?

From *Songs for Parents,* by John Farrar. Reprinted by arrangement with the publishers, Yale University Press.


# MEETING THE EASTER BUNNY

### Rowena Bastian Bennett

*All*
On Easter morn at early dawn before the cocks were crowing,
*Solo 1*
I met a bob-tail bunnykin and asked where he was going.
*Solo 2*
" 'Tis in the house and out the house a-tipsy, tipsy toeing,
*Solo 3*
'Tis round the house and 'bout the house a-lightly I am going."
*Boys*
"But what is that of every hue you carry in your basket?"
*Girls*
" 'Tis eggs of gold and eggs of blue;
*Solo 4*
I wonder that you ask it.

*Girls*
'Tis chocolate eggs and bonbon eggs
*Boys*
And eggs of red and gray,
*All*
For every child in every house on bonny Easter Day."
*Row 1*
He perked his ears
*Row 2*
And winked his eye
*Row 3*
And twitched his little nose;
*Row 4*
He shook his tail——
*Solo 5*
What tail he had——
*Row 5*
And stood up on his toes.
*Solo 6*
"I must be gone before the sun;
*Boys*
The East is growing gray;
*Girls*
'Tis almost time for bells to chime."
*All*
So he hippety-hopped away.

From *Songs from Around a Toadstool Table*. Reprinted by permission of Wilcox and Follet Company, publishers.

## BIRTHDAYS

### Marchette Gaylord Chute

*All*
We had waffles-with-syrup for breakfast,
*Boys*
As many as we could hold;
*Solo 1*
And I had some presents extra,
Because I am six years old.

*Solo 1*
I've thanked everyone for my presents,
    *Girls*
And kissed 'em, and now that's done
*All*
The family's all ready to do things,
*Solo 1*
Whatever I think would be fun.

*Boys*
When Timothy had his birthday
*All*      *Girls*
We went to the circus, and Tim
Laughed so hard at the seals and monkeys
*All*
That a real clown winked at him.

*Solo 2*
And Dorothy chose a picnic
*Row 1*
On the shore of a little lake,
*Row 2*   *Row 3*   *Row 4*
With tadpoles, and buns, and diving,
*All*
And a four-layer birthday cake.

*Solo 1*
And now that it's my turn for choosing,
I'm going to ask if we might
*Row 5*
Take all our family of rabbits
    *All*
To bed with us, just for tonight.

Reprinted from *Rhymes About Ourselves,* by Marchette Gaylord Chute. By permission of The Macmillan Company, publishers.

# TRANSPORTATION

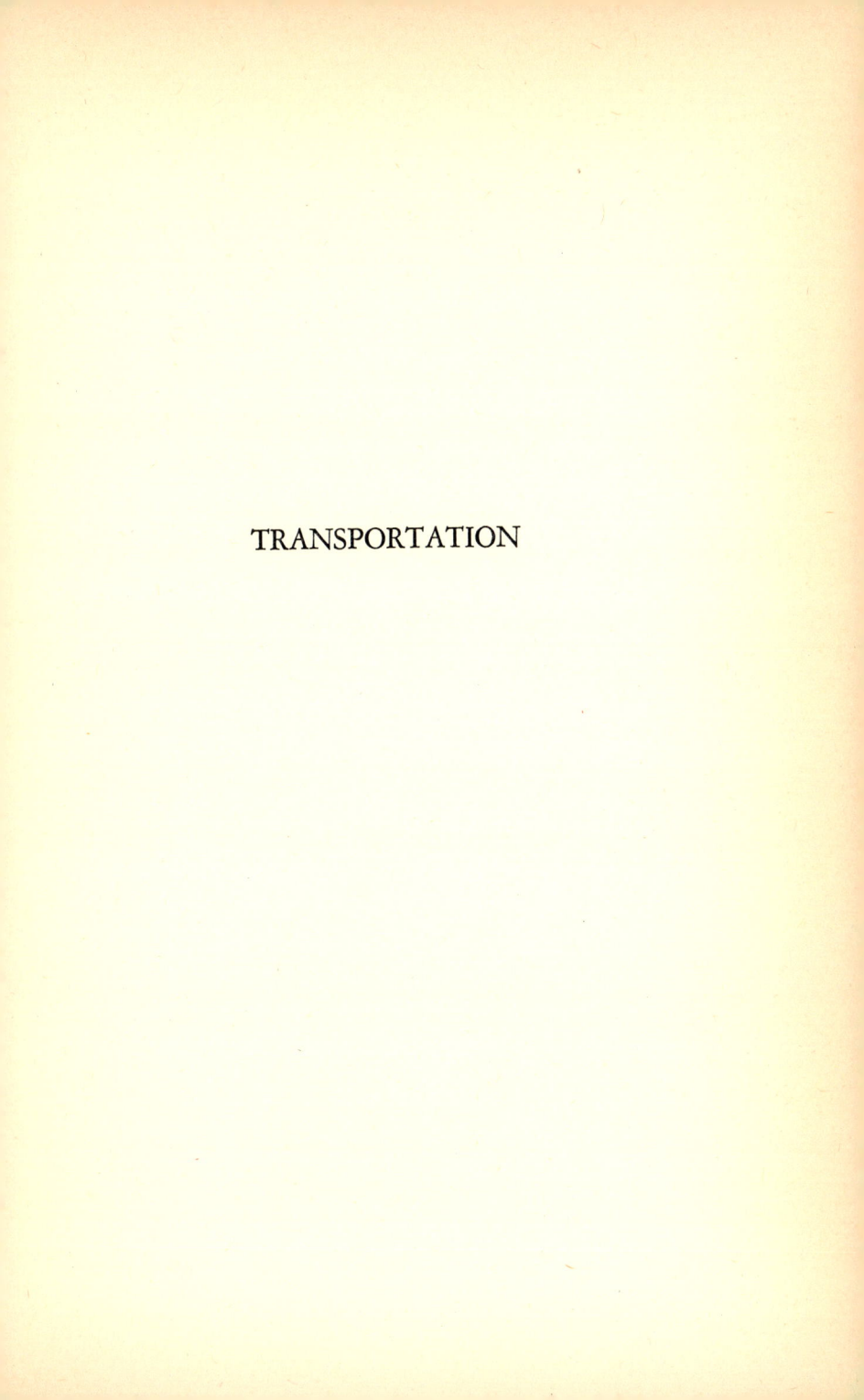

# FUNNY THE WAY DIFFERENT CARS START

### Dorothy Baruch

*Solo 1*
Funny the way different cars start.
*Row 1*
Some with a chunk and a jerk,
*Row 2*
Some with a cough and a puff of smoke
Out of the back,
*Row 3*
Some with only a little click—
With hardly any noise.

*Solo 2*
Funny the way different cars run.
*Row 4*
Some rattle and bang,
*Row 5*
Some whirrr,
*Row 6*
Some knock and knock.
*Girls*
Some purr
*Boys*
And hummmmm
*All*
Smoothly on with hardly any noise.

Reprinted by special permission of the author, and of Harper and Brothers, publishers.

# ENGINE

### James S. Tippett

*Solo 1*
I wonder if the engine
That dashes down the track
*All*
Ever has a single thought
Of how it can get back.

*Girls*
With fifty cars behind it
*Boys*
And each car loaded full,
*Solo 2*
I wonder if it ever thinks
*All*
How hard it has to pull.

*Solo 3*
I guess it trusts the fireman;
*All*
It trusts the engineer;
*Solo 4*
I guess it knows the switchman
*All*
Will keep the tracks clear.

From *I Go A'Traveling*, by James S. Tippett. Copyright, 1929, by Harper and Brothers.

# STOP—GO

### Dorothy Baruch

*All*
Automobiles
In a row
*Girls*
Wait to go
*Boys*
While the signal says:
*Solo*
STOP.

*All*
Bells ring
Ting-a-ling!
*Girls*
Red light's gone!
*Boys*
Green light's on!
*Girls*
Horns blow!
*Boys*
And the row
*All*
Starts to
GO.

Reprinted from *I Like Automobiles,* by Dorothy Walter Baruch, by permission of the John Day Company, Inc. Copyright by Dorothy Walter Baruch, Oct. 29, 1931.

WEE FOLKS AND MAGIC

# FAIRIES

### Hilda Conkling

*Solo 1*
I cannot see fairies,
*All*
I dream them.
*Solo 2*
There is no fairy can hide from me;
*All*
I keep on dreaming till I find him:
*Solo 3*
There you are, Primrose!—
*Solo 4*
I see you, Black Wing.

From *Poems by a Little Girl,* by Hilda Conkling. Copyright, 1920, by J. B. Lippincott Company, and reprinted by their permission.


# FAIRIES

### Marchette Gaylord Chute

*Solo 1*
You can't see fairies unless you're good,
*All*
That's what nurse said to me.
*Girls*
They live in the smoke of the chimney,
*Boys*
Or down in the roots of a tree;
*Girls*
They brush their wings on a tulip,
*Boys*
Or hide behind a pea.

*All*
But you can't see fairies unless you're good,
*Solo 2*
So they aren't much use to me.

From *Rhymes About Ourselves,* by Marchette Gaylord Chute. Reprinted by permission of The Macmillan Company, publishers.

# FAIRY AEROPLANES

### Annie Blackwell Payne

*Girls*
The fairies, too, have aeroplanes
*All*
To carry them about,
*Boys*
That swoop, and soar, and dart, and dip,
*All*
And circle in and out.

*Girls*
So when their little wings are tired,
*All*
They summon one of these,
*Boys*
And sail above the garden beds
*All*
Or anywhere they please.

*Boys*
The fairies' aeroplanes are safe
And never do capsize,
*Girls*
They're very beautiful and gay,
*All*
Because they're butterflies.

Reprinted by courtesy of The Parents' Institute, Inc.


# THE FAIRY BOOK

### Abbie Farwell Brown

*All*
When Mother takes the Fairy Book
And we curl up to hear,
*Solo 1*
'T is "All aboard for Fairyland!"
*All*
Which seems to be so near.

*Boys*
For soon we reach the pleasant place
Of Once Upon A Time,
*Girls*
Where birdies sing the hour of day,
*Solo 2*
And flowers talk in rhyme;

*Boy*
Where Bobby is a velvet Prince,
*Girl*
And where I am a Queen;
*Solo 5*
Where one can talk with animals,
*Solo 6*
And walk about unseen;

*Boys*
Where Little People live in nuts,
*Girls*
And ride on butterflies,
*All*
And wonders kindly come to pass
Before your very eyes;

*Girls*
Where candy grows on every bush,
*Boys*
And playthings on the trees,
*All*
And visitors pick basketfuls
As often as they please.

*Girls*
It is the nicest time of day—
*Solo 7*
Though bedtime is so near,—
*Boys*
When Mother takes the Fairybook
*All*
And we curl up to hear.

Reprinted by special arrangement with the author and Houghton Mifflin Company, publishers.

# THE LITTLE ELF

### John Kendrick Bangs

*Solo 1*
I met a little Elf-man, once,
*Girls*
Down where the lilies blow.
*Solo 2*
I asked him why he was so small,
*Boys*
And why he didn't grow.

*Girls*            *Boys*
He slightly frowned, and with his eye
*Solo 3*
He looked me through and through,
*Solo 4*            *Solo 5*
"I'm quite as big for me," said he,
*All*
"As you are big for you."

From *St. Nicholas Book of Verse*, copyright, 1923, by the Century Company. Reprinted by permission of Appleton-Century-Crofts, Inc.

# FAIRY SHOES

### Annette Wynne

*All*
The little shoes that fairies wear
Are very small indeed;
*Boys*
No larger than a violet bud,
*Girls*
As tiny as a seed.

*All*
The little shoes that fairies wear
Are very trim and neat;
*Boys*
They leave no tracks behind for those
Who search along the street.

*Girls*
The little shoes of fairies are
So light and soft and small,
*Solo*
That though a million pass you by
*All*
You would not hear at all.


## RING-A-RING

### Kate Greenaway

*Boys*
Ring-a-ring of little boys,
*Girls*
Ring-a-ring of girls;
*All*
All around—all around,
Twists and twirls.

*Teacher*
You are merry children.
*All*
"Yes, we are."
*Teacher*
Where do you come from?
*All*
"Not very far.

*Girls*
"We live in the mountain,
*Boys*
We live in the tree,
*Solo*
And I live in the river bed
*All*
And you won't catch me."

Reprinted by permission of Frederick Warne and Company, Inc., publishers.

# PLEASE

### Rose Fyleman

*Boys*
Please be careful where you tread,
*Girls*
The fairies are about;
*Solo 1*
Last night, when I had gone to bed,
I heard them creeping out.
*Row 1*
And wouldn't it be a dreadful thing
To do a fairy harm?
*Row 2*
To crush a little delicate wing
*Row 3*
Or bruise a tiny arm?
*Solo 2*
They're all about the place, I know,
*All*
So do be careful where you go.

*Row 4*
Please be careful what you say,
*Row 5*
They're often very near,
*All*
And though they turn their heads away
They cannot help but hear.
*Row 6*
And think how terribly you would mind
If even for a joke,
*Boys*
You said a thing that seemed unkind
*Girls*
To the dear little fairy folk.
*Solo 2*
I'm sure they're simply everywhere
*All*
So promise me that you'll take care.

From *Fairy Green*, by Rose Fyleman. Copyright, 1923, by Doubleday and Company, Inc.

# THE RAINBOW FAIRIES

### Lizzie M. Hadley

*Boy and Girl*
Two little clouds one summer's day
*All*
Went flying through the sky.
*Girls*
They went so fast they bumped their heads,
*All*
And both began to cry.

*Boys*
Old Father Sun looked out and said,
*Boy*
"Oh, never mind, my dears,
I'll send my little fairy folk
To dry your falling tears."

*Solo 1*
One fairy came in violet,
*Solo 2*
And one in indigo;
*Solo 3   Solo 4  Solo 5   Solo 6    Solo 7*
In blue, green, yellow, orange, red,
*All*
They made a pretty row.

*Girls*
They wiped the cloud's tears all away,
*Boys*
And then, from out the sky
Upon a line the sunbeams made,
*All*
They hung their gowns to dry.

Reprinted by permission of Walter McLaughlin, executor.

# SNOW FAIRIES

## Isla Paschal Richardson

*Solo 1*
I watched a little snowflake
Come sailing from the sky,
It played a joke on me when
It fell right in my eye.

*Girls*
Another little snowflake
Came dancing toward the south,
*All*
It looked at me a minute—
*Solo 2*
Then landed in my mouth!

*Girls*
They seemed like little fairies
Upon a holiday,
*Boys*
Just out for fun and frolic
*All*
And asking me to play.

Reprinted from *The Instructor*, with permission from F. A. Owen Publishing Company.

# INDEX

About Buttons, 33

Baa, Baa, Black Sheep, 17
Birches, The, 95
Bird's Nest, 61
Birthdays, 142
Blessing Over Food, 133
Boots, Boots, Boots, 47
Bridges, 33
Bundles, 141

Catkin, 96
Chickens, The, 61
Child's Grace, A, 133
Clouds, 117
Cover, 95
Crescent Moon, 97
Crickets, 62
Cupboard, The, 32

Dandelion, The, 97
Dandelion, The, 98
Dandelions, 116
Dewdrop, A, 96
Ding Dong Bell, 25
Duck, The, 64

Echo, 34
Engine, 148
Evening Hymn, 134
Everybody Says, 35

Fairies, 153
Fairy Aeroplanes, 154
Fairy Book, The, 154
Fairy Shoes, 156
Familiar Friends, 65
Farmer Went Riding, A, 17
Fireflies, 66
First Snow, 99
Five Years Old, 40
Frozen Milk Bottles, 98
Funny the Way Different Cars Start, 147

Galoshes, 35
Goldfish, The, 66
Good Morning, 67
Goosie Gander, 18
Growing Up, 36

Hair Ribbons, 47
Halloween Meeting, A, 137
Hey Diddle Diddle, 19
Hickory Dickory Dock, 17
Hiding, 36
Hippity Hop to Bed, 56
House Cat, The, 69
Humpty Dumpty, 19

Ice, 109
Icicle, The, 100
Icy, 39
I Had a Little Pony, 19
I Love Little Pussy, 68
I Wonder, 101

Jack and Jill, 20
Jack Frost, 114

Kitten's Night Thoughts, 70
Kitty, The, 71

Little Bo-Peep, 21
Little Boy Blue, 21
Little Bug, 63
Little Dreamer, The, 57
Little Elf, The, 156
Little Jack Horner, 22
Little Miss Muffet, 22
Little Plant, The, 99
Little Turtle, The, 88
Lucy Locket, 23
Lullaby, 39

Mary Had a Little Lamb, 24
Mary Middling, 73
May Morning, 119
Meeting the Easter Bunny, 141
Merry-Go-Round, 38
Merry Sunshine, 104
Mice, 72
Milk in Winter, 101
Milking Time, 41
Milkman's Horse, The, 74
Mistress Mary, 23
Mitten Song, The, 103
Mix a Pancake, 25
Moon, The, 102
Moon, The, 104
Moon, So Round and Yellow, 113

Moral Song, 74
Mother, 127
Mouse, 73
Mrs. Brown, 128
Mrs. Peck-Pigeon, 69
Mud, 42
My Dog, 75
My Funny Umbrella, 42
My Kite, 44
My Policeman, 129
My Shadow, 43
My Valentine, 138
My Zipper Suit, 44

Naughty Little Robin, The, 77
Naughty Soap Song, 45
New Baby Calf, The, 78
New Shoes, 45

Old King Cole, 26
Once I Saw a Little Bird, 76
One, Two, Buckle My Shoe, 20

Park, The, 46
Pat-a-Cake, 30
Patrick Goes to School, 126
Pease Porridge Hot, 28
Pigeons, The, 78
Playing Leaves, The, 118
Please, 158
Pop Corn Song, A, 49
Precocious Piggy, 82
Pussy Willow, 115

Quarrelsome Kittens, The, 84

Rabbit, The, 80
Rabbits, 87
Rain, 100
Rain, 103
Rain in the Night, 112
Rainbow Fairies, The, 159
Raindrops, 109
Raining, 105
Riddle: What Am I?, 140
Ride-A-Cock Horse, 24
Ring-A-Ring, 157
Robin, 81
Robin, The, 86
Rocking Horse, 48
Runaway Brook, The, 114

Secret, The, 51
Secret, The, 139
See-Saw, 50
Seesaw, 51
"Sh," 52
Sing a Song of Sixpence, 27
Skyscrapers, 53
Sleep, Baby, Sleep, 125
Smells (Junior), 54
Sneezing, 55
Snow, 110
Snow Fairies, 160
Snowflakes, 107
Snowflakes, 108
Snowman, The, 110
Snowstorm, 111
Soap Bubbles, 54
Some Little Mice, 27
Spinning Top, 55
Sprinkling, 46
Squirrel, The, 85
Stop—Go, 148
Swallow, The, 85

There Was a Crooked Man, 28
Three Little Kittens, 90
Time to Rise, 89
To Baby, 125
Tom, Tom, the Piper's Son, 23
Tracks, 63
Tragedy, The, 106
Troubles, 48
Twinkle, Twinkle, Little Star, 116

Under the Ground, 118

Was She a Witch, 137
What Does Little Birdie Say?, 89
When Blue Sky Smiles, 113
When I Was a Little Boy, 29
When Santa Claus Comes, 140
Where Do All the Daisies Go?, 120
Whistle, 56
White Window, The, 120
Who's In, 57
Why Do the Bells of Christmas Ring?, 138
Wild Beasts, 88
Wise Johnny, 111
Woodpecker, The, 91

162